THE
SUPER BOWL
AN OFFICIAL RETROSPECTIVE

EDITED BY KEN LEIKER AND CRAIG ELLENPORT

Published in the United States by Ballantine Books,
an imprint of The Random House Publishing Group,
a division of Random House, Inc., New York.

Ballantine and colophon are registered trademarks of
Random House, Inc.

Cataloging-in-Publication Data is available from the
Library of Congress upon request.

ISBN 0-345-487192

Printed in the United Kingdom

www.ballantinebooks.com

First Edition: November 2005

9 8 7 6 5 4 3 2 1

Designed by Rare Air Media

PHOTO CREDITS

Walter Iooss, Jr.
Pages 9, 18, 19, 21, 36, 38, 44, 45, 48, 70, 71, 76 (2), 77, 80 (9), 81, 82-83, 84, 85 (3), 86, 87, 88, 89 (2), 92, 93, 95, 99, 102, 103, 203

Tony Tomsic, *US Presswire*
Pages 2-3, 6-7, 8, 9, 11, 22, 34, 35, 46 (2), 52, 59 (2), 72 (2), 79, 92, 112, 114, 144 (2), 145, 146, 148, 149, 153, 154, 165, 168, 169

US Presswire
Pages 15, 23, 24, 24, 39, 59, 60, 63 (2), 72, 84, 145, 161, 162, 164, 172, 174-175, 176, 181, 191, 212-213

Focus On Sport, *Getty Images*
Pages 14, 76, 76 (3), 101, 105, 122, 126, 128, 129, 130, 131, 179, 198, 199, 204

Malcolm Emmons, *US Presswire*
Pages 8, 10, 42, 68, 69, 84, 92, 144, 150, 157 158, 173, 176, 192-193, 197

Mike Powell, *Allsport, Getty Images*
Pages 20, 25, 26, 28-29, 67, 72, 85, 89 (3), 108, 210-211

Andy Lyons, *Allsport, Getty Images*
Pages 1, 18, 36, 44, 50, 54-55, 61, 75, 94, 113, 178, 186-187

Rick Stewart, *Allsport*
Pages 26, 40, 89, 97, 109, 134, 179 (2)

Brian Bahr, *Getty Images*
Pages 8, 16-17, 74, 179, 183, 185, 188, 204, 214-215

Al Bello, *Getty Images*
Pages 13, 30, 62, 70, 94 (3), 105, 138, 171

Michael Zagaris, *Getty Images*
Pages 56, 57, 58, 64, 65, 194 (2)

Stephen Dunn, *Allsport, Getty Images*
Pages 24, 37, 94 (2), 128, 170, 179

Jonathan Daniel, *Allsport, Getty Images*
Pages 53, 84, 94, 167, 179, 205

Otto Greule, *Allsport, Getty Images*
Pages 37, 70, 89, 90, 94

George Gojkovich, *Getty Images*
Pages 84, 85 (2), 132

Frank Micelotta, *Getty Images*
Pages 13, 180, 184, 195

Doug Pensinger, *Allsport*
Page 177, 179, 206-207, 208-209

Rhona Wise, *AFP, Getty Images*
Pages 104, 136, 137, 191

Donald Miralle, *Getty Images*
Pages 9, 13 62

National Football League
Pages 184, 185 (2)

Diamond Images, *Getty Images*
Pages 41, 126

Tony Duffy, *Getty Images*
Pages 104, 106

Elsa, *Getty Images*
Pages 50, 71

Jose Carlos Fajardo, *Contra Costa Times, Zuma Press*
Pages 182, 183

Getty Images
Pages 118, 119

Jeff Haynes, *AFP, Getty Images*
Pages 176, 195

Jed Jacobsohn, *Getty Images*
Pages 72, 183

Preston Mack, *US Presswire*
Pages 143, 191

Bob Gomel, *Time Life Pictures, Getty Images*
Page 12

Heinz Kluetmeier, *Time Life Pictures, Getty Images*
Page 12

The Sporting News Archive, *Zuma Press*
Page 14

Ronald Martinez, *Getty Images*
Page 19

Bud Symes, *Getty Images*
Page 20

Dilip Vishwanat, *US Presswire*
Page 24

Harry How, *Getty Images*
Page 31

Hulton Archive, *Getty Images*
Page 33

George Silk, *Time Life Pictures, Getty Images*
Page 47

Robert Seale, *The Sporting News, Zuma Press*
Page 51

David Drapkin, *Getty Images*
Page 74

Jeff Gross, *Getty Images*
Page 74

Time Life Pictures, *Getty Images*
Page 77

Kidwiler Collection, *Diamond Images, Getty Images*
Page 78

Joe Patronite, *Allsport*
Page 94

Lonnie Major, *Allsport*
Page 117

Bruce Bennett Studios, *Getty Images*
Page 119

NFL Photos, *Getty Images*
Page 141

Bob Leverone, *The Sporting News, Zuma Press*
Page 142

Brian Lowe, *Keystone Pictures*
Page 172

C.A. Record, *Charlotte Observer, Zuma Press*
Page 183

by Luciano Borsari, *Zuma Press*
Page 184

Scott Gries, *Image Direct*
Page 189

Doug Kanter, *AFP, Getty Images*
Page 192

Rick Stewart, *Getty Images*
Page 171

Tom Hauck, *Getty Images*
Page 171

Todd Warshaw, *Getty Images*
Page 171

If the opportunity to create this book came out of nowhere, then the help came from everywhere. In a process that started less than four months before the book was completed, the efforts of those involved went far beyond what might otherwise be expected.

At the NFL, Craig Ellenport worked a daunting schedule, which no doubt coincided with the one he handles day-to-day, and never blinked. Kind, considerate, and committed, Craig helped us through the wonder that is the National Football League while shaping this book. None of this would have been possible without his considerable contributions from the first moment to the last.

Greg Aiello, whose reputation for excellence preceded him, made sure we were on the right path all the time. The fact that he found time to review the smallest nuance speaks to his commitment and kindness.

Michael Capiraso and Shandon Melvin jumped off a mountain of work to contribute their creative talents and insight to the cover design.

Vic Carucci and Ray Didinger went from a phone call to research and writing in what seemed like the same moment. As they have done throughout their distinguished careers, each came through on target and on time.

At NFL Films, Chris Willis couldn't have been more helpful; his assistance and insight can be seen throughout these pages. Hal Lipman guided us through the DVD production, and Jeanne Diblin and Kathy Davis helped us navigate.

Ken Leiker proved yet again to be an immense talent with a focus and integrity all his own. He came on board at a moment's notice and didn't get off until the last word was right. This book could not have happened in the timeframe, much less at the level it was created without Ken's tireless efforts.

The third leg of the project was John Vieceli, who grabbed hold of the graphic design and made it his own. He searched for the best photography, designed and redesigned pages, made adjustments, constantly refined, and never once complained, despite far too many days that ran deep into far too many nights. John managed the hardest job with the skill of a consummate professional.

At VSA Partners, Curt Schreiber helped us get started and provided much needed assistance all the way through.

At Ballantine Books, Gina Centrello, Anthony Ziccardi, Bill Takes, Jennifer Osborne, Katherine Malloy, Carl Galian and Mark Maguire were once again wonderful partners. Anthony and Bill turned on a moment's notice and made it all happen, and Jennifer assisted us at every stop as only she can. It remains a pleasure to work with each of them.

At Home, my beautiful wife, Laura, and our amazing children, Alexandra, Samantha, Isabella and Jonah, gave of themselves so I could work with all these wonderful people. They remain the best of me.

Special thanks: Chris Russo, Walter Iooss, Jr., Richard Renno, Silas Munro, Amy Lany and Nick DeCarlo.

Mark Vancil
President
Rare Air Media

CONTENTS

Raising
the Curtain

"In my day, the $12,000 to $15,000 they paid for the Super Bowl was a lot of money. For some players, it matched their salary, and for other players, it was at least two-thirds of their salary. The money was fine; the ring was fine. But I was 22 years old, and the important thing for me was playing the Green Bay Packers. And now as I get older than dirt, it's even more important that I can say, 'I played in that first one.' It was very, very exciting to play in the first one."

MIKE GARRETT, *running back, Chiefs*

DOUBT, FEAR AND ANXIETY PERMEATED THE NATIONAL FOOTBALL LEAGUE HIERARCHY IN THE EARLY DAYS OF 1967.

WILL THEY COME?

WILL THEY WATCH? WILL THEY CARE?

Pete Rozelle was not yet being hailed a consummate sporting visionary. Rozelle, the NFL commissioner at the time, merely hoped that his legacy would not include a line that read: Creator of a colossal bust. "Go back to the first Super Bowl, and all I can remember is 30,000 empty seats," Rozelle told reporters 19 years later, two days before Super Bowl XX.

About 62,000 fans were in the 100,000-seat Los Angeles Memorial Coliseum when the Green Bay Packers, champions of the National Football League, and the Kansas City Chiefs, champions of the American Football League, met on January 15, 1967, in what was called the "First World Championship Game." It wouldn't officially be known as the Super Bowl for several years. Rozelle certainly had no reason to believe that the Packers' 35-10 victory over an opponent from an upstart league would serve as a magnet for more fans in the stands and additional television viewers the next time the game was played.

No one, including Rozelle, could have envisioned how significant an event the Super Bowl would become. The NFL marks its signature game in Roman numerals, and the February 5, 2006, edition is XL, which also is a measure of size. In truth, the Super Bowl long ago outgrew Extra Large. XXL or XXXL is more fitting.

Tickets for Super Bowl I were priced at $8, $10 and $12. Now, they cost $600 and $700, and the demand far exceeds the supply. The 10 most-watched television programs in history are

"There were actually three Super Balls

that were given by my wife to our three children at that time, Lamar Jr., Sharon and Clark. It was a highly concentrated rubber ball manufactured by the Wham-O company. You could bounce this ball off of concrete, and it would literally bounce over a house. The kids were always talking about these Super Balls. I think that's how the name came about.

In the fall of 1966, in one of our joint committee meetings between the AFL and the NFL, we were talking about where we were going to have this championship game. One of the people said, 'Which game are you talking about?' I said,

'Well, you know, the last game after the last game. The final game. The championship game. The Super Bowl.'

The members of the committee—three of us from the AFL, three from the NFL, and Pete Rozelle—all kind of looked at me, and we all kind of smiled. Thereafter, the committee began to refer to the game as the Super Bowl. It was three or four years before the league itself officially adopted that name, but the media and the public seized on it. Especially when CBS and NBC promoted that first game as 'Super Sunday: Watch our broadcast.'"

LAMAR HUNT, *owner, Chiefs*

Super Bowls. The game is televised in more than 100 countries, and broadcast in 31 languages, including English, Spanish, Dutch, Italian, French, German, Japanese, Portuguese and Russian. About 3,000 journalists from around the world cover the game annually.

The Super Bowl should not be regarded as merely a game or an event. "It has become an American holiday. Like the Fourth of July in [winter]," says NFL commissioner Paul Tagliabue.

Says Phil Simms: "As a kid, you dream about playing in the Super Bowl. The reality is even better than the dream." Simms, an NFL analyst for CBS, was selected the Most Valuable Player of Super Bowl XXI for leading the New York Giants to victory over the Denver Broncos.

Consider this bit of global perspective from Paul McCartney, one of the world's best-known entertainers and the featured halftime performer at Super Bowl XXXIX: "There's nothing bigger than being asked to perform at the Super Bowl."

Len Dawson,
on SUPER BOWL I

"The Kansas City Chiefs against the Green Bay Packers at Super Bowl I, they said, 'Well, it's kind of a Mickey Mouse league, the AFL, and lots of teams in the NFL can beat the Chiefs.' That was Lombardi talking after Super Bowl I. We had to live with that for seven months, and the team that really paid was the Chicago Bears. The following year we had preseason games against the NFL before the final merger came in 1970, and we put 66 points on the board in a preseason game against Dick Butkus, Gale Sayers, George Halas and the Chicago Bears. That's the emotion that's involved in losing a Super Bowl.

That was the worst defeat in the history of George Halas as a coach. Abe Gibron was an assistant with the Bears, and he had gone to Purdue, and so had Hank Stram, our coach, and two of our assistants, Pete Brewster and Tom Bettis, and I had, too. Before the game we're talking, and Abe says, 'Well, it's just a scrimmage, a little preseason game. No big deal. We're not going to throw too much at you.'

Well, we'd been waiting seven months to get our revenge for losing to the Packers. And after we had scored 66 points, Abe ran up to Hank Stram and says, 'You shouldn't have done that. You're going to kill the old man'—meaning Halas."

skeptical public wasn't the only reason for the many empty seats at the first Super Bowl. The NFL had only two months to promote the game once the President signed a Congressional bill authorizing the merger of the NFL and AFL.

There were early signs of the Super Bowl's potential. After the Packers beat the Dallas Cowboys for the NFL championship, Jim Kensil, the league's executive director at the time, traveled to Los Angeles to promote Super Bowl

a dozen people were in attendance, and the collection basket contained little money, according to Kensil. A week later, the morning of the game, he returned to the church, and this time it was full, along with the collection basket. That was perhaps the NFL's first graphic evidence of the Super Bowl's economic impact on the host city.

Super Bowl economics have reached astounding proportions. A 30-second TV commercial costs more than $2 million. Keenly aware of the vast viewing audience, Super

I and soon was fielding many telephone inquiries about tickets and media credentials in his room at the Los Angeles Hilton. Though pleasantly surprised by the interest, Kensil moved to another hotel room—in the name of his brother-in-law—so he could get some sleep.

A week before the game, Kensil attended Catholic services at a small church in downtown Los Angeles. About

Bowl advertisers try to outdo each other with creative and memorable commercials that sometimes become part of American television lore. Indeed, day-after discussion about Super Bowl commercials competes with talk about the game itself.

New England Patriots quarterback Tom Brady has played in three Super Bowls and twice been selected the game's

"That first year, the Packers stayed up in Santa Barbara. We had a media bus going up, taking the writers. In those days, it was not radio and TV reporters, just writers. We did that Tuesday, Wednesday, Thursday and Friday. We also sent the bus up to Santa Barbara the day before the game, and only one person was on the bus. It was Jack Hand, who worked for the Associated Press. Nice guy. It was him and the bus driver—one reporter going up to interview the Packers, the whole entire team, the day before the first Super Bowl. We sure have grown since those days.

Now, we have media day on Tuesday at the stadium, and we may have 600 or 700 people there. Wednesday and Thursday, we have mass interviews, and by that time we'll have 800 to 900, radio/TV/print, in there.

It's become a status thing with the players that they have to have their own table so that the media can gather around. You put the quarterback at his own table, and the running back. When you get down to some of those defensive linemen and the fifth defensive back, we probably won't give them an entire table. We might ask them to split it, and have two defensive backs at one table. They get upset because they want to have their own table. Even if no one comes over to interview them, they'll want to have their own table so that they look big-league in the eyes of their teammates."

JOE BROWNE, *NFL Executive VP, Communications*

MVP, yet he continues to be awe-struck by the game's mass appeal. "It's huge," Brady says. "Every single sporting eye in the world is focused on that game.

"Going into the media tents, you see every single writer, from every single magazine and newspaper, that you've always read stories from. Every TV show is focused on the match-ups of the game and how they're

going to play out. The Goodyear blimp ... the painting on the field... the way your jersey looks—it all takes on new meaning.

"Before the team runs out onto the field, when you're sitting in front of your locker, that's when it dawns on me. That's when I say, 'Holy ----! This is what it all comes down to.' It's unlike any other game you ever play.

"One thing I really liked about our team was that we did realize what was going on. We felt that we were doing some great things, and let's enjoy and savor those moments. We did it on and off the field. Some things only happen once in a lifetime. A lot of football players never get to the Super Bowl; some only once. We went four times. When we went the first time, it was so good and so wonderful, we said, 'We have to do this again,' and it just kept getting better. That was a wonderful feeling, not getting tired of the Super Bowl."

FRANCO HARRIS, *running back, Steelers*

"The feeling that you get running onto the field for that game is indescribable. There's no other thing I've found I can do in my life that can measure up to that. There's so much excitement and energy in your body. It's the greatest rush of emotion that you could ever have."

Adds Simms: "When you're getting ready to take the field for that first Super Bowl, you say, 'Oh, my God! I'm going to pass out

just trying to run out of the tunnel.'

"The biggest thing I tried to accomplish in the two weeks before the game was make sure that emotions would not be a factor in my play. Basically, that's all Bill Parcells, our coach, and Ron Erhardt, our offensive coordinator, talked about with me. When you get too excited as a quarterback, you'll miss an open receiver and do something you normally don't do."

"Winning's a very precious thing, and to be called the champion, it's why we do these things. I'm not naïve enough to think that it represents anything substantial in the spectrum of things in this world. But in this particular industry, the NFL, it does mark the pinnacle, and for those that get there, it's a very special thing. It's something that you keep with you forever."

BILL PARCELLS, *coach, 1986 and 1990 Giants, Super Bowl champions*

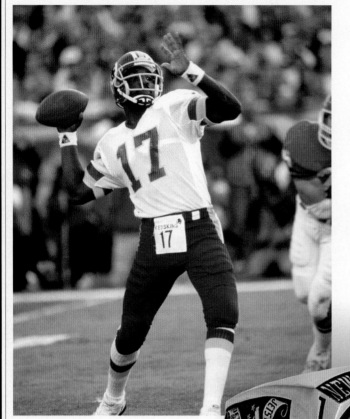

rolled-up papers clenched in his fist, celebrating as Len Dawson and the rest of the Kansas City Chiefs upended the Minnesota Vikings in IV. There is sharp-chinned Don Shula on the sideline, tersely watching the final seconds tick away in Super Bowl VII as his Miami Dolphins completed the NFL's only perfect season. There is stone-faced Tom Landry, peering out from under his signature fedora as quarterback Roger Staubach guided the Dallas Cowboys to Super Bowl glory.

Who can forget Terry Bradshaw flinging long pass after long pass to Lynn Swann and John Stallworth as the Pittsburgh Steelers established their dynasty? Or professorial Bill Walsh, arms folded, watching Joe Montana, the coolest of characters, connect with Jerry Rice and John Taylor as the San

H eroes and legends are made at the Super Bowl.

Vince Lombardi guided the Green Bay Packers to convincing victories in Super Bowls I and II—they won five NFL titles in his nine seasons as coach—and now the Tiffany trophy that is awarded to the game's winner bears his name. In beating the Baltimore Colts in Super Bowl III, Joe Namath and the New York Jets registered one of the greatest upsets in sports history. As Namath trotted off the field waving his index finger, he was doing more than reaffirming the Jets' accomplishment—he was signaling the arrival of the AFL as a worthy partner with the NFL.

Namath's finger-waving is among Super Bowl images that continue to linger. There is beefy-faced Hank Stram,

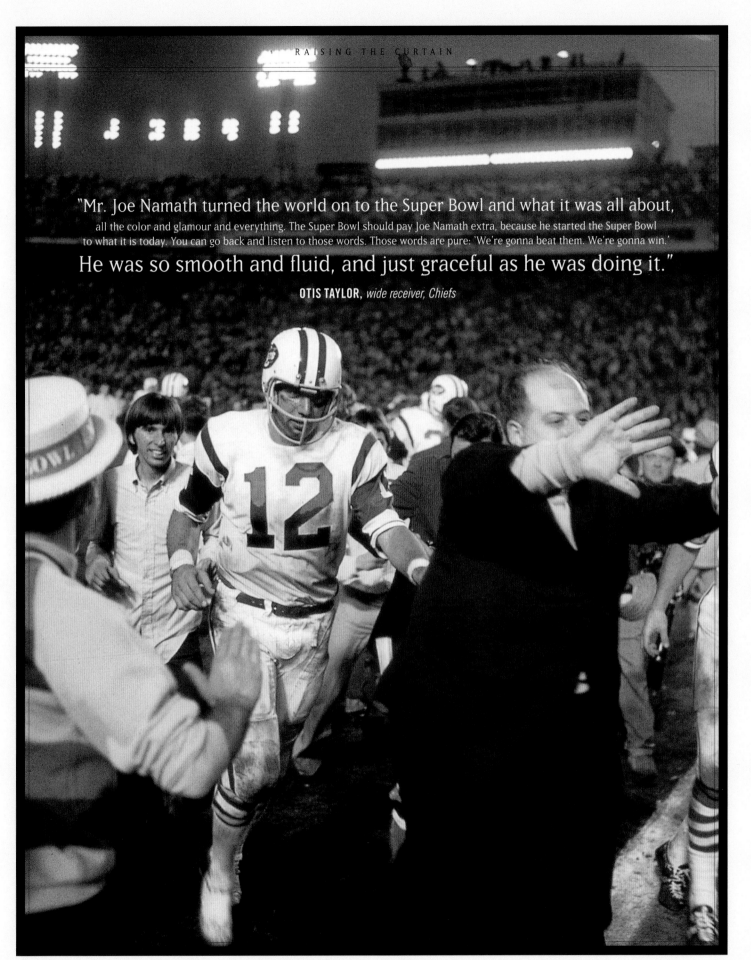

"Mr. Joe Namath turned the world on to the Super Bowl and what it was all about, all the color and glamour and everything. The Super Bowl should pay Joe Namath extra, because he started the Super Bowl to what it is today. You can go back and listen to those words. Those words are pure: 'We're gonna beat them. We're gonna win.' He was so smooth and fluid, and just graceful as he was doing it."

OTIS TAYLOR, *wide receiver, Chiefs*

"One night Jim Hudson, our strong safety, and I were going to have dinner with Dan Sullivan, the starting offensive guard, and Lou Michaels, defensive end and kicker, of the Baltimore Colts. We're at the bar and restaurant in Fort Lauderdale called Fazio's, and I did not bring the game up. But Lou came up with this thing about how, 'We're going to kick your ---.' I said, 'Lou, come on. We're just going to eat. Why would you say that?'

He said, 'I'll tell you why. Because something goes wrong, we got the man that can come in and do it'—meaning Johnny U. Now, I wore number 19 in high school, and my nickname was Joey U., so I liked Johnny U., too. But I said, 'Hey, Lou, c'mon. What are you talking about, man? We both know Johnny can't throw across the street right now. His arm hurts; he's got a bad arm.' And I said, 'Besides that, Lou, what the heck do you know? You're nothing but a damn kicker.'

Woo, boy—Lou's jaw was going square, and he stood up. About that time, three tuxedos stepped in and said, 'Calm down, guys. Calm down.' Lou and I exchanged a few words, and then we sat down and had dinner together.

A night later, I went to the Miami Touchdown Club to get an award from the AFL. I got up to the podium, and about the time I'm getting ready to talk, a guy in the back of the room goes, 'Hey, Namath, we're gonna kick your ---.' I said, 'Whoa, whoa, wait a minute.' I'd just had it by then. 'You guys have been talking for two weeks now'—meaning the Colts fans and the media—'and I'm tired of hearing it.'

I said, 'I got news for you: We're going to win the game. I guarantee it.' It was just out of anger and frustration. Our defense wasn't getting any credit for being the best. Our team was the 19-point underdog, after we had just beaten the Raiders, whom I thought was an outstanding team. You know how you hear complaining all the time about, 'We get no respect.' Well, we weren't getting respect. And that's how the guarantee came out. It was not planned. It wasn't premeditated. I really believed we were going to win the game.

The next morning when I saw Coach Ewbank, it dawned on me that I had said possibly the wrong thing. Coach Ewbank says, 'Look what you've done. You've gone and given these guys fuel to get fired up.' He said, 'Here we've got them believing they're the best team in the world. For two weeks, everybody is patting them on the back, shaking their hands. They think they've already got the game won. And you go ahead and give them the material to get fired up.'

He was right, and I was wrong. But I didn't mean to, and I told him I didn't mean to. But I also told him if they needed those clippings to get fired up, they were in big trouble. And that's the way it turned out."

JOHNNY UNITAS

Francisco 49ers carved out a dynasty of their own? Or Joe Theismann, Doug Williams and Mark Rypien, the quarterbacks of Joe Gibbs' three Washington Redskins teams that won the Super Bowl?

How about behemoth William "The Refrigerator" Perry, normally a defensive tackle, lining up at running back and plowing in for a touchdown for the Chicago Bears? Or Emmitt Smith churning out yardage as the Cowboys became the team of the 1990s? Or John Elway winding down a brilliant career in back-to-back Super Bowl victories, after enduring three Super Bowl losses in his callow youth? Or Adam Vinatieri calmly kicking last-second field goals that gave the Patriots their first two Super Bowl triumphs?

Some players are remembered almost exclusively for the Super Bowl. Jim O'Brien's lone moment of fame came when he kicked the field goal that gave the Colts a 16-13 victory over Dallas in Super Bowl V. Larry Brown's career is defined by the MVP award he won in Super Bowl XXX for twice intercepting Neil O'Donnell passes and helping the Cowboys beat the Steelers. Desmond Howard was selected

"You answer the question time and time and time and time again:

Will your career be complete if you don't win the Super Bowl?

From 1990 until 1998, that's a lot of times to be asked that. When John Mobley knocked down that fourth-down pass of Brett Favre's, I will always remember seeing that ball hit the ground and realizing that we were finally, finally world champions. I felt like the world was taken off my shoulders. I felt that my career was legitimized."

JOHN ELWAY, *quarterback, Broncos*

"Probably the most disturbing thing in my career was people saying,

'Wow! You didn't give the ball to Walter Payton to score in the Super Bowl.'

If I had one thing to do over again, I would make sure that he took the ball into the end zone.
I was fortunate enough to score a touchdown in the Super Bowl. He can have mine. They can take mine
out of the record book and give it to Walter. I'm sure it bothered him, because the greats want to
perform at that level in the biggest game of their career."

In Their Words

The Chicago Bears were leading the New England Patriots, 37-3, late in the third quarter of Super Bowl XX
when rookie defensive tackle William "The Refrigerator" Perry scored on this 1-yard run.

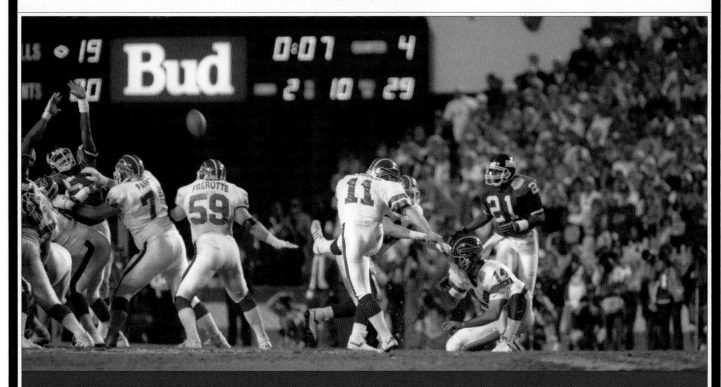

"When I've seen it in the past, and if I see it in the future, it's the same—it's always going to be wide right. That's the thing about our past: You can't make it any better; you can't make it any worse. So I've simply moved on and tried to be the best I could be in trying to prepare for the next kick.

I felt bad about it, but I was comfortable that I had done the best that I could do. I always prepared, worked hard. I could always look at myself in the mirror and know that I did my best."

SCOTT NORWOOD, *kicker, Bills*

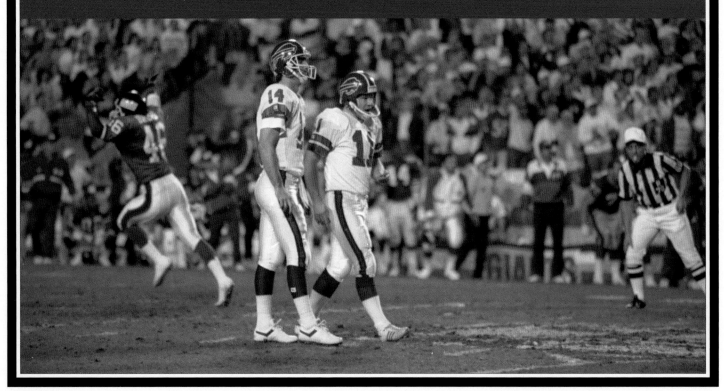

"On the plane back after the game, I recalled a poem that was in a slim volume of English poetry that my mother had given me way back when I had joined the Army Air Corps during World War II. It was by an unknown British poet in the 15th century about a Scottish warrior. It went just four lines:

Fight on, my men, Sir Andrew said.
A little I'm hurt, but not yet slain.
I'll just lie down and bleed awhile.
Then I'll rise and fight again.

I had that typed up and blown up and posted on the bulletin board for the next day, when the players came in for the team meeting. After the meeting, about eight to ten players asked me if they could get a copy of it. Three or four times after that, whenever we'd had a particularly discouraging moment, or a game that we felt badly about losing, somebody—I don't know who—put that poem back up on the board."

MARV LEVY, *coach, Bills*

the MVP of Super Bowl XXXI for a 99-yard kickoff return for a touchdown that helped the Packers beat the Patriots.

"You can't get any higher than being crowned MVP of the Super Bowl. Not in our profession," Howard wrote in the book, *Super Sunday.* "You have MVPs of the league every year. But to be MVP of the Super Bowl … is just a blessing. It's something that only a few people can boast. Especially people who do what I do, which is return punts and kicks."

Adds Simms: "I don't know if I would have ever gotten the chance to be an announcer if I weren't the MVP of a Super Bowl. You have to have the big moments behind you to give you credibility with the fans and with the people who hire and fire people who do this job."

Super Bowl failure is just as long lasting. Scott Norwood is remembered for missing a 47-yard field goal attempt in the final seconds of the Buffalo Bills' 20-19 loss to the Giants in Super Bowl XXV. Norwood and his wife continue to be approached by people who talk about his miss as if it just happened.

The Super Bowl defines teams and the men who play for them. Win four in a decade, as the Steelers did in the 1970s and the 49ers in the 1980s, and you are declared a dynasty. Lose four in a row, as the Bills did in the early 1990s, and you become a national symbol for second-best. "Whoever wins gets that Super Bowl trophy," Brady says. "And whoever loses, nobody ever remembers who they are, or hardly remembers."

Dynasties notwithstanding, the Super Bowl remains a realistic goal for all 32 NFL teams. Consider the Baltimore Ravens, who had records of 4-12, 6-9-1, 6-10 and 8-8 in successive years, and then won Super Bowl XXXV after posting a 12-4 record during the 2000 regular season. "Our system gives every team the same chance, and it gives the fans serious hope that their team can make the playoffs and make a run at the Super Bowl championship," Tagliabue says.

"To win a Super Bowl, it is not simply a matter of who

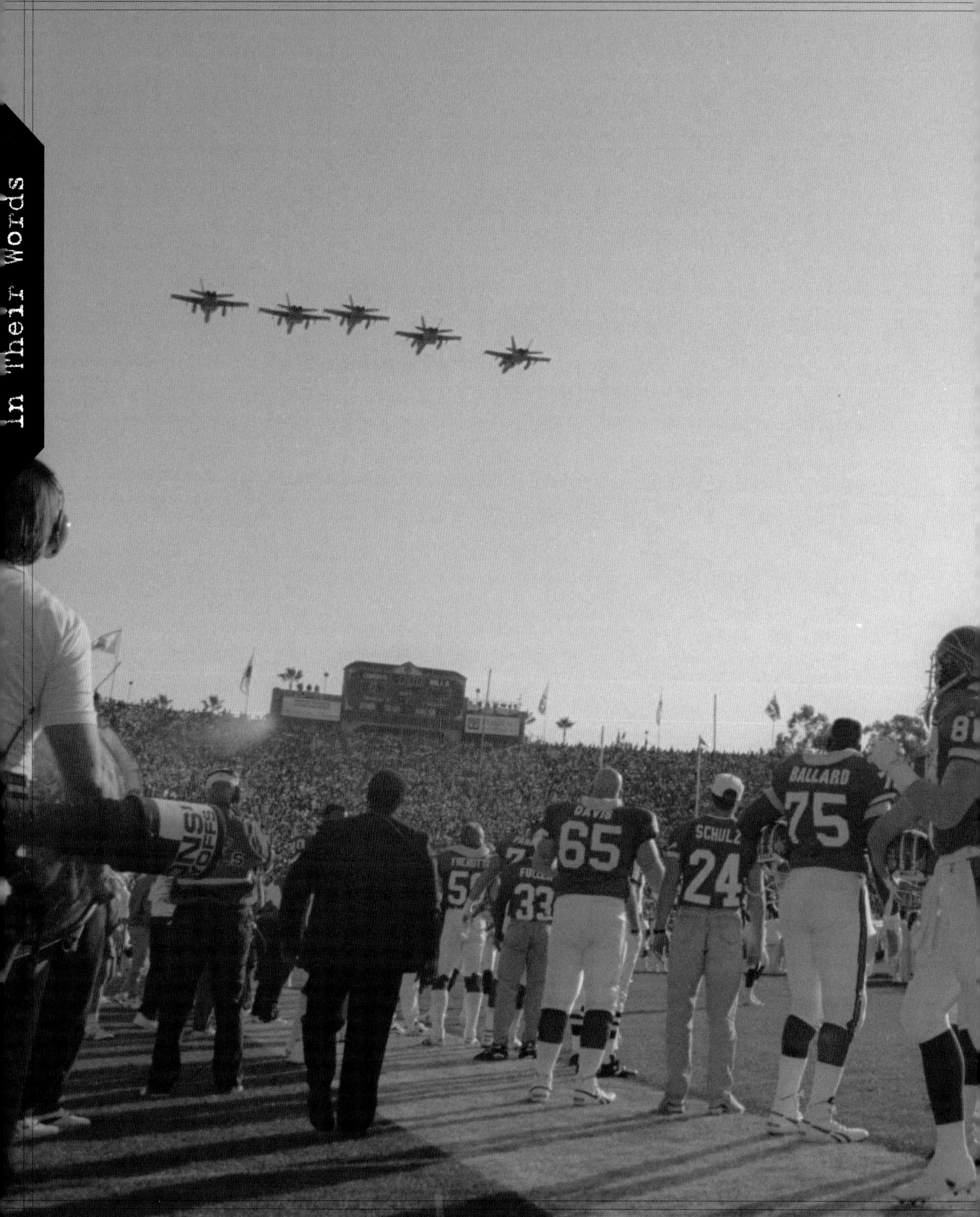
DAVIS 65
SCHULZ 24
BALLARD 75
33

"In 1987, my senior year in high school, I was named the Gatorade national football player of the year.

With that recognition, I was awarded two tickets to the Super Bowl in Pasadena, two airline tickets, all accommodations taken care of. I took my high school quarterback, Johnny Nichols, who was my best friend. We're out there in the Rose Bowl watching the Giants and the Broncos. Man, it was just full of excitement. I turned to John and said, 'One day I'm gonna play in the Super Bowl, and I'm gonna play it right here.'

Six years later, the Cowboys are playing in the Rose Bowl against Buffalo, and Johnny Nichols is sitting up in the stands. He remembered my statement as if it was yesterday. I was out on that field, and it was one of the most exciting experiences any man can ever have. When them jets flew over, wow! Man, that stadium was rocking. It was time to play ball."

"Norman Vincent Peale had a quote: 'If Jesus were alive today, he'd be at the Super Bowl.'
That's probably an accurate statement. It really is that kind of game. When you hear people in casual
conversation, people who aren't necessarily sports fans, who want to make an analogy about
something big, they'll say, 'Boy, this is like the Super Bowl of pastry contests,' or, 'This is Super Bowl
of travel agents' conventions.' It's become the metaphor for everything that's huge and important.
If somebody wants to drive home the point that this is as big as it gets, they say, 'This is the
Super Bowl of whatever.' I think that pretty much tells you all you need to know."

RAY DIDINGER, *sportswriter*

had the most money, who is in the biggest city, or just having one great play. It is a matter of who has an organization that can compete, build a team from top to bottom, put a lot of talent together, and have that talent work as a team."

Has the Super Bowl gotten too big? Perhaps. Or maybe the weeklong extravaganza serves a greater purpose than just determining a championship. As Rozelle observed as he watched the game grow from modest beginnings to

"In a society that is becoming more and more fragmented, in which people don't watch the same things on television the way we all watched *I Love Lucy* and *The Ed Sullivan Show*, the Super Bowl gives us a moment when we all do come together for a good reason. Not to watch something political; not to watch a tragedy. But just to come together on this level of friendship, and share something and enjoy it. That's wonderful and that's dear, in a way. One does not usually think of football as dear and precious. But what it does to America by binding us for that time, even if you don't give a hoot about football, is good."

FRANK DEFORD, *sportswriter and author*

resounding success: "If the American public didn't have an entertaining, emotional outlet, we'd have trouble. We'd be a sick society. I don't say the Super Bowl is the end of the world. But we feel it gives half the country the chance to think of something else other than our domestic problems, our international problems.

"It's meant to be fun, and we think it is."

STARR

When the Green Bay Packers represented the NFL in the first Super Bowl, which was not even known as the Super Bowl at the time, how could we possibly have known this annual championship game would grow into the extraordinary global event it is today? However, there were some clues that this was the start of something big.

Packers coach Vince Lombardi had a great appreciation of history, so he did an excellent job conveying the importance of this first-ever title game between the NFL and the fledgling American Football League.

As for any sense of what this game might become in the overall landscape of sports and American culture in general, there was no way to know. There was nothing we could fall back on as a reference. Except for this: While we had been privileged to play in five NFL championship games over a seven-year span, we had never, ever seen as many people from the national media as were there for the first NFL–AFL Championship Game in Los Angeles on January 15, 1967. It was a strong signal, and unreal at that time. Obviously it pales in comparison with today, but in those days it was very large and very significant.

There was just as much pressure then as there is now. It was a unique experience. We were honored and thrilled to be representing the prestigious National Football League in the first game of its kind. For Coach Lombardi, it was a matter of pride. Many fans didn't think the AFL could compete with the best the NFL had to offer, but as we prepared for the game, it was obvious to us that the Kansas City Chiefs were a very good football team.

We had a lot of respect for the Chiefs, and it was not a surprise that the game was very close in the first half, closer than most remember, since the

final score was 35–10. We were a great football team, but so were they. The biggest difference was our experience in championship games, and in the second half it became obvious.

Even after that incredible media blitz, it wasn't until a few years down the road that we began to appreciate the size and importance of the Super Bowl. In the years following our appearances in Super Bowls I and II, we were privileged to attend future Super Bowls. We saw the crowds—and the intensity—grow to mammoth proportions. It was a wonderful experience.

The Super Bowl started as a battle for pride. We knew the Chiefs were worthy opponents, as were the Oakland Raiders in Super Bowl II. Because the Packers were fortunate enough to prevail in those games, however, the AFL and its fans still had something to prove.

Joe Namath and the Jets changed all that in Super Bowl III, and it was with mixed emotions that I watched that historic contest. As an NFL man, I was naturally disappointed to see the mighty Baltimore Colts defeated. I was personally pleased for Namath, a fellow University of Alabama alum. What Namath and the Jets accomplished was an eye-opener for most of the NFL.

Anyone who thought Super Bowl III was a fluke would soon be proved wrong. The Chiefs beat the Minnesota Vikings a year later to win Super Bowl IV. Some people were stunned that the AFL had won two Super Bowl titles, but remember the respect we had for that league when we faced the Chiefs and Raiders.

The NFL and AFL would then merge, and I really believe the Super Bowl has grown significantly over the years because of the combined strength of both conferences. Everything surrounding the Super Bowl has grown—the publicity, the celebrity factor, the halftime shows—and it has added to the mystique of Super Sunday. It is quite an event, and everyone associated with professional football should be very proud. I still believe the level of competition is the driving force behind the Super Bowl's popularity.

Football is the greatest example of a team sport. There is no other sport in which you have 11 players working together at one time as a team. It is the ultimate team sport, and that is what makes the Super Bowl the ultimate championship event.

Coach Lombardi was right when he told us it would be a significant honor to be crowned champion of the first title game of its kind. It was just as special a few years later, when the trophy given to the Super Bowl champion was named in Lombardi's honor. I'm sure I can speak for all of our players who were there at the time. We were privileged to have been led and coached by him.

The official attendance at the Los Angeles Memorial Coliseum for Super Bowl I was 61,946, but the number of fans who tell me they were there seems to be ten times that number. For those of us who were there, it's certainly something we'll never forget.

Guiding Lights

Don Shula likes to tell the story about dining at a Honolulu restaurant in 1993 with Bill Walsh, Chuck Noll and George Seifert. The coaches were in Hawaii for the Pro Bowl. Shula was coaching the AFC team and Seifert the NFC squad. Walsh and Noll had recently been selected to the Pro Football Hall of Fame.

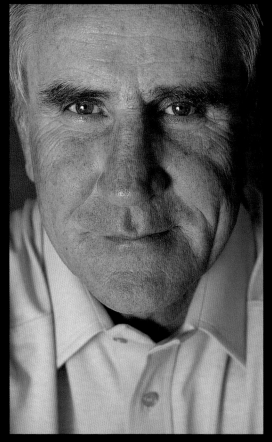

"We started counting up Super Bowl wins," Shula says. "Chuck Noll was the champ; he was 4-0. Walsh was 3-0. Seifert was 1-0 [and would improve to 2-0]. Then came my turn. I was embarrassed to say I was 2-4. I was the only loser in the bunch."

Shula's lament notwithstanding, loser is a word that hardly is associated with his name—he won more games than any other coach in NFL history. Shula was merely commenting on the perception that winning the Super Bowl is the ultimate mark of a coach's greatness.

Teams come to mind when discussing Super Bowl dynasties (Green Bay, Pittsburgh, San Francisco, Dallas and New England);

upsets (New York Jets over Baltimore, Kansas City over Minnesota, Denver over Green Bay and New England over St. Louis); and great finishes (Baltimore over Dallas, San Francisco over Cincinnati, New York Giants over Buffalo, St. Louis over Tennessee, New England over St. Louis and New England over Carolina). But no one receives more credit for victory—or blame for loss—than the head coach. Fair or not, his is usually the most lasting face, voice and, especially, mind attached to the outcome.

Winning the Super Bowl more than once makes a coach a "genius." Losing the Super Bowl more than once makes him a coach who "can't win the big one." Perhaps no coach carries a heavier burden

than Dan Reeves, whose 0-4 record (three with the Denver Broncos and one with the Atlanta Falcons) casts a dark shadow on an otherwise impressive résumé. Worse for Reeves, the Broncos won the Super Bowl five years after he departed, and repeated that achievement the next season when they beat his Falcons. John Elway was the Broncos quarterback when they lost Super Bowls under Reeves and won them under Mike Shanahan.

The stigma of losing the Super Bowl has not kept great coaches from being duly noted and immortalized. Marv Levy, who suffered four consecutive Super Bowl losses with Buffalo, and Bud Grant, who went 0-4 with Minnesota, are

in the Hall of Fame.

Yet one has to wonder if the Tiffany trophy presented to the Super Bowl champion would bear the name of Vince Lombardi had his championship run with Green Bay ended with the three NFL titles he won and not continued with victories in the first two Super Bowls, against Kansas City and Oakland. By defeating the Chiefs and the Raiders in convincing fashion, Green Bay expanded its dominance over two leagues, the NFL and the AFL, and Lombardi gained at least a slight edge over another coaching icon of the same era, Paul Brown, who led Cleveland to seven NFL championship games (and three titles) but never made it

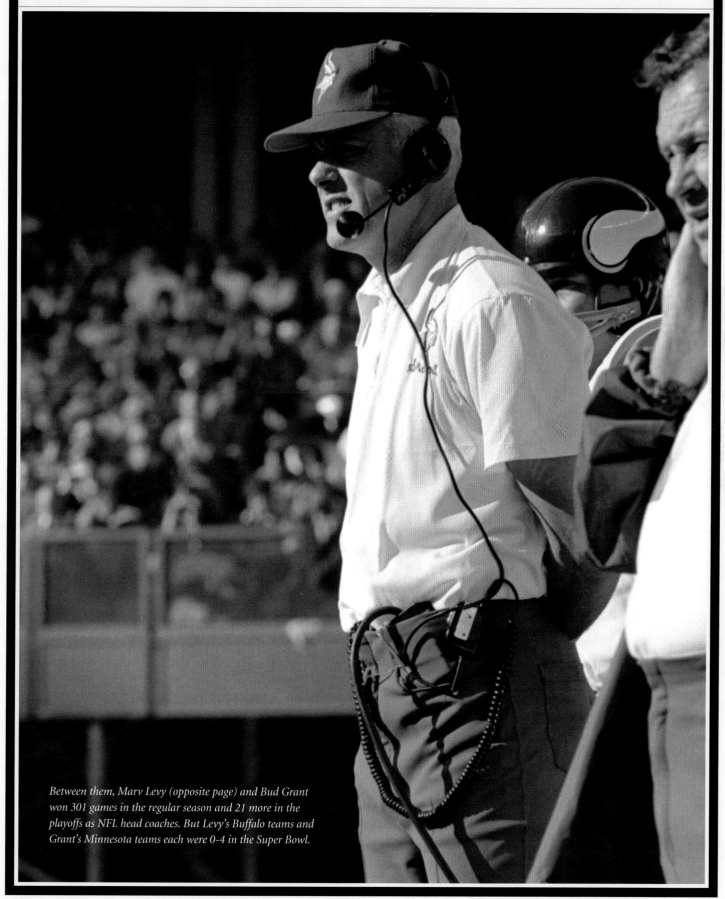

Between them, Marv Levy (opposite page) and Bud Grant won 301 games in the regular season and 21 more in the playoffs as NFL head coaches. But Levy's Buffalo teams and Grant's Minnesota teams each were 0-4 in the Super Bowl.

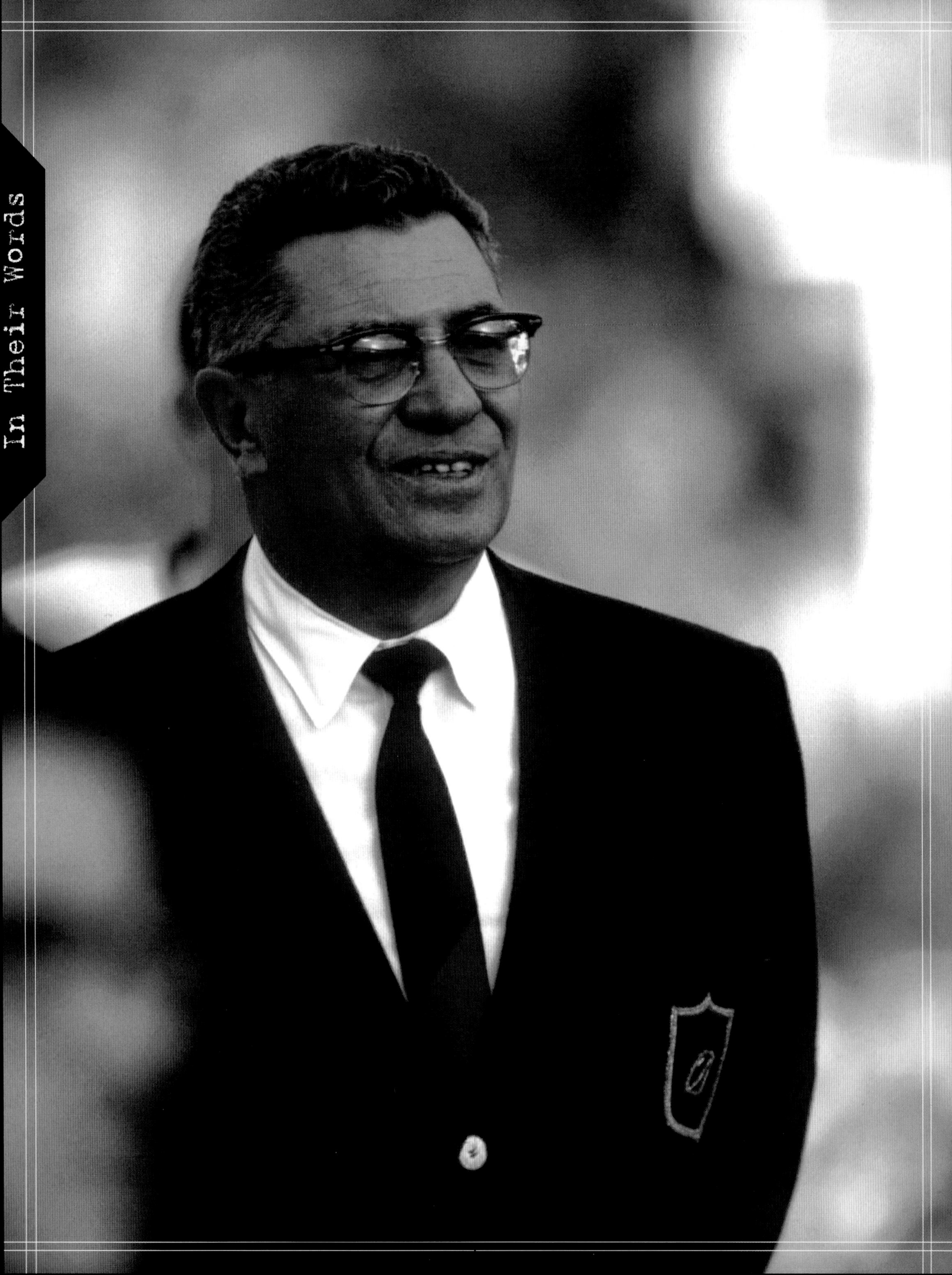

"My first encounter with Coach Lombardi was at what today would be called a minicamp. He had just been hired, and he brought a number of us in to acquaint us with his offensive system. After about an hour we took a break. I ran to the Packers office building and grabbed the pay phone and called my wife back in Alabama.

'Honey, we're going to win,' I said to her.

We could've taken a break after 20 minutes, and I could've made the same phone call—it was that obvious. The way he approached it, his organizational skills, the charisma of him standing in front of you teaching, all of it was so engaging. Listening to him, I was so excited I probably wasn't even touching the chair I was sitting in.

We had the core of a good football team, but what we lacked was leadership. From the time he began to speak, it was obvious that we now had that leadership. He brought that the day he walked in the front door.

We were much better organized and we were much better prepared because of his leadership and teaching. He took great pride in teaching. He said that coaching was the epitome of teaching. We began to grow very rapidly in his system."

to a Super Bowl.

In some cases, the Super Bowl has embellished coaching careers that otherwise might be remembered as being ordinary. Noll won only 57 percent of his games in Pittsburgh. Joe Gibbs had only 140 victories in his first stint with the Washington Redskins (1981 to 1992), but three Super Bowl victories helped him earn a bronze bust in the Hall of Fame, the same measure of immortality accorded the likes of

Shula (347 wins) and George Halas (318 and six NFL championships).

For years, Bill Belichick lived in the considerable shadow of Bill Parcells, who coached the New York Giants to two Super Bowl victories. Belichick, Parcells' defensive coordinator, devised brilliant game plans, including the scheme that stopped Buffalo's formidable no-huddle offense in Super Bowl XXV and later was taken to the Hall of Fame for display.

"The thing I'm impressed with, more than anything, is the way Bill Belichick handled the 2003 season. He had a lot of injuries. He had a lot of situations he had to overcome, but you never heard any excuses. You never heard him complaining about anything."

DON SHULA, *coach, 1972 and 1973 Dolphins, Super Bowl champions*

SUPER BOWL COACHES: MOST VICTORIES

FOUR

CHUCK NOLL, PITTSBURGH

THREE

BILL BELICHICK, NEW ENGLAND
JOE GIBBS, WASHINGTON
BILL WALSH, SAN FRANCISCO

TWO

TOM FLORES, OAKLAND/LA RAIDERS
JIMMY JOHNSON, DALLAS
TOM LANDRY, DALLAS
VINCE LOMBARDI, GREEN BAY
BILL PARCELLS, NEW YORK GIANTS
GEORGE SEIFERT, SAN FRANCISCO
MIKE SHANAHAN, DENVER
DON SHULA, MIAMI

Belichick became the head coach of the Browns, but was dismissed after five seasons, a 36-44 regular season record and 1-1 mark in the playoffs casting much doubt about his ability to be the team leader.

Given another chance, Belichick thrived. In leading the Patriots to three Super Bowl victories in four seasons, he gained a place among the greatest coaches in history. His 10-1 postseason record is first on the all-time list. For strategizing in Xs and Os and assembling an efficient organization, Belichick is as good as there is, and arguably as good as there ever has been. His Patriots teams are renowned for getting meaningful production from everyone on the roster.

"The thing I'm impressed with, more than anything, is the way he handled the 2003 season," Shula says of Belichick's work after the Patriots beat Carolina for their second Super Bowl victory. "He had a lot of injuries. He had a lot of

Coach Weeb Ewbank (above) and the New York Jets handed Don Shula his worst day on a football field. But Shula later had two Super Bowl victories to celebrate.

"You damn well better not let that Mickey Mouse [American Football] league beat you. It'd be a disgrace, a complete, utter disgrace."

VINCE LOMBARDI, *coach, Packers*

"A lot of my thinking on how I ought to carry myself as a leader in my company comes from the example that Chuck Noll set for us. I don't know that I consciously think that I'm doing this or that like Chuck did, but at the end of a day or the end of a week, I might look back on some things that I hold dear and realize they are the same things that Chuck endeavored to teach us as part of that football team. Things like:

'You never arrive. You never get to the point that you're the best you can possibly be.'

Chuck always preached that we needed to get better; and that you got better one step at a time, one day at a time, one game at a time. That's a philosophy that works in any endeavor.

The other thing about Chuck: From an integrity standpoint, he was beyond reproach. If you want anything to last for a long time, if you want to build something for the long haul, I think integrity has to be the cornerstone. Chuck was an excellent example of that."

situations he had to overcome, but you never heard any excuses. You never heard him complaining about anything. All you did was see him plug people into certain situations, and these guys responding to that opportunity, and they somehow found a way to win. A lot of that has to do with coaching."

Belichick assembled an extraordinarily talented staff of assistant coaches, including offensive coordinator Charlie Weis and defensive coordinator Romeo Crennel. After the Patriots defeated the Philadelphia Eagles in Super Bowl XXXIX, Weis left to become the head coach at Notre Dame and Crennel was hired as head coach of the Browns.

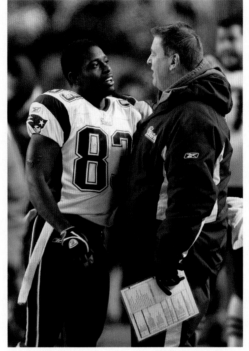

Typical of the assistants' contributions to the Patriots' success was Weis' work in his final game with New England. After the offense struggled to handle Philadelphia's relentless blitzing in the first quarter, Weis used the Eagles' aggressiveness against them. He deployed four-receiver formations and called for screen passes that were especially effective because the linebackers and safeties were not in position to defend them, and the cornerbacks were occupied in coverage. The Patriots scored touchdowns on three of their next five drives.

"In the four years I've been quarterbacking, I can't remember him calling a screen out

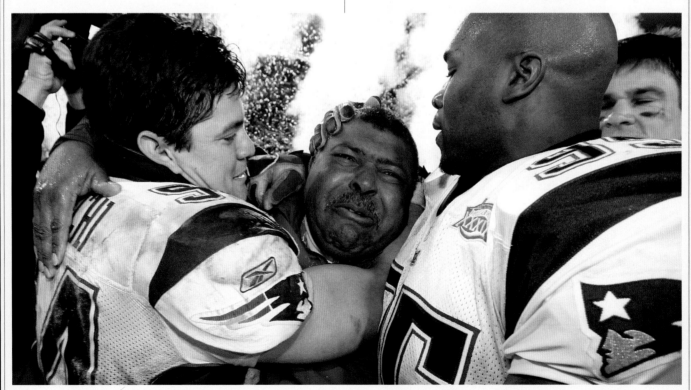

New England players embraced the wisdom of the team's Super Bowl coordinators, offensive mastermind Charlie Weis (top) and defensive guru Romeo Crennel (above).

of a four-wide formation," quarterback Tom Brady says. "But that's Charlie—expect the unexpected."

A coach's behavior can do plenty to influence the demeanor of his team entering a game, and history shows that is especially true in the days leading to the Super Bowl. If the game's magnitude causes the head coach to become uptight—a seemingly natural response—his players are

biggest week of their careers.

Vermeil's approach was a stark contrast to the ultra-loose style of Tom Flores, the coach of the Eagles' opponent, the Raiders. Oakland quarterback Jim Plunkett said that he and some teammates cruised the French Quarter on the team's first night in New Orleans, and didn't spot a single Eagles player. Flores also had an 11 p.m. curfew, but at least one

Tom Flores won Super Bowl championship rings as a player, assistant coach and head coach. His Raiders won Super Bowl XV and XVIII.

apt to follow suit. If he projects himself as being relaxed, his players probably will react accordingly. For contrasting styles, consider Super Bowl XV and XVI.

In XV, Dick Vermeil kept the Philadelphia Eagles in virtual lock-down at the team's New Orleans hotel, which was near the airport and far from the party atmosphere of Bourbon Street. He strictly enforced an 11 p.m. curfew and maintained a rigid approach to practice and meetings. Some players privately grumbled that they couldn't enjoy the

of his players, John Matuszak, was spotted dancing in the Quarter well past midnight. Vermeil said he would have put Matuszak on the next flight home, just as he would any curfew violator. Said Raiders offensive guard Gene Upshaw, "If he coached us, he'd look up and down the sideline and see that he was all alone."

On the day of the game, the Eagles seemed tense and uneasy while the Raiders appeared calm and relaxed. Final score: Oakland 27, Philadelphia 10.

In XVI, Bill Walsh arrived in Pontiac, Michigan, ahead of his 49ers. He played a trick on his players by disguising himself as a bellman and greeting them at the hotel with a prediction that they were going to "get their butts kicked" by the Cincinnati Bengals.

The 49ers won, 26-21. What Walsh's prank might have had to do with the outcome is debatable, although a coach known

Vermeil gave a much longer address to the St. Louis Rams, whom he had transformed from an also-ran to a contender in three seasons, before they defeated the Tennessee Titans, 23-16, in one of the most dramatic Super Bowl finishes ever.

"We don't have to be anything different than we really are," Vermeil told his squad. "We are here because of what we are and what we've done. Everything we've done and

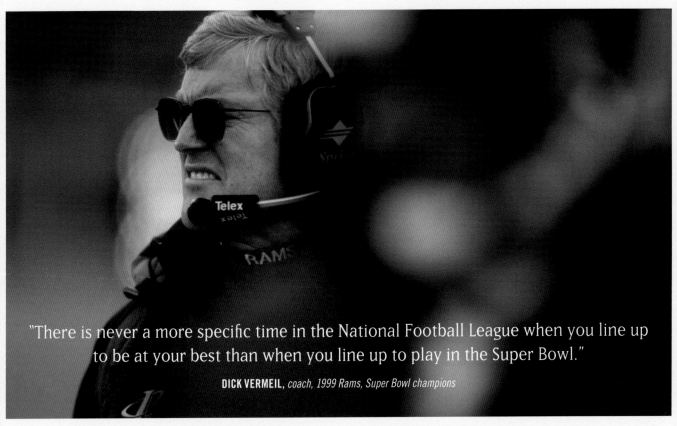

"There is never a more specific time in the National Football League when you line up to be at your best than when you line up to play in the Super Bowl."

DICK VERMEIL, *coach, 1999 Rams, Super Bowl champions*

for his offensive brilliance gained additional respect from his players for setting a carefree tone for the Super Bowl.

Coaches have delivered some inspiring messages to their players before the Super Bowl. One of the shortest, and surely the most threatening, came from Lombardi before his Packers pounded the Raiders, 33-14, in Super Bowl II: "You damn well better not let that Mickey Mouse [American Football] league beat you. It'd be a disgrace, a complete, utter disgrace."

overcome in the last three years was a hell of a lot bigger challenge than what we face on the football field today. Granted, the stakes are higher, and the pressure to win greater, but isn't that why we worked our butts off for three years to get here? This is what we wanted all along.

"We are very capable of winning this football game. And I expect to win. So do you. All we have to do is be at our best … just like we planned to be all year."

Then came Vermeil's big finish: "There is never a more

Willie McGinest, on BILL BELICHICK

"Coach Belichick is here all the time. He sleeps here almost every night.
He's a mad scientist when it comes to breaking down teams. He makes it simple
for us. He gives us two or three things that we must do to win that week.
If we play good football—that's his main thing, to play good football, eliminate
the bad plays, and we concentrate on those two or three things and do them
right—then nine times out of ten we'll win the game.

Every week something changes. There's always something new, and there's
always a little twist to it. Right when you think you've figured him out or you
understand him, there's something else he pulls out of the bag."

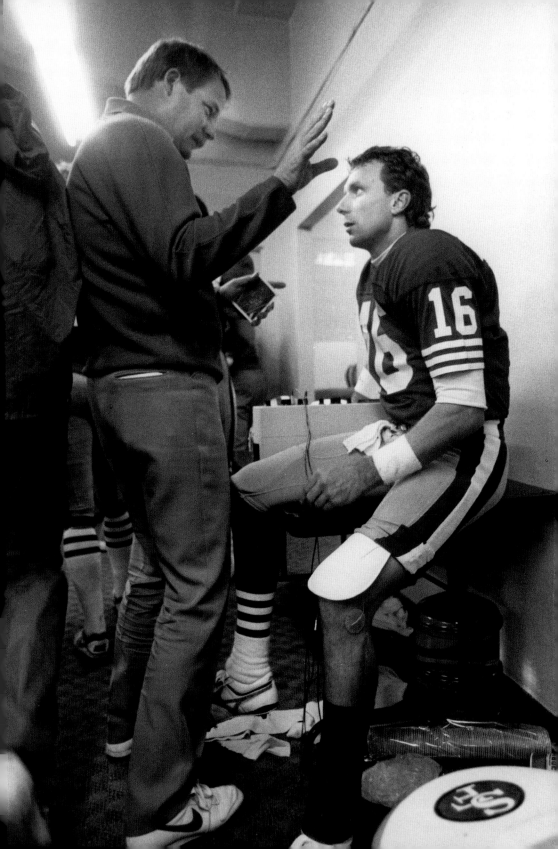

specific time in the National Football League when you line up to be at your best than when you line up to play in the Super Bowl."

Surprisingly, there has never been a memorable halftime speech in a Super Bowl locker room. "If anything, during the Super Bowl you want to go in the other direction," says Mike Shanahan, who guided Denver to its back-to-back Super Bowl wins. "You want a calming atmosphere because the players are jacked anyhow. They know how important it is, so if anything you've got to approach it more that this is another game."

Levy says, "The players have been put through a wringer all week and through the first half. Almost the last thing you need at halftime is some contrived pep talk."

There is plenty of time for one, if not an entire lecture series. For regular season games, halftime lasts 12 minutes.

To accommodate a Super Bowl halftime show, the break lasts at least twice as long. As a semi-serious Shanahan says, it is long enough to "put in a whole new game plan." He never had the urge to do that, considering the Broncos were ahead at the half in both of their Super Bowl victories.

A challenge for every Super Bowl coach is to use the extra time wisely. Coaches can cover far more strategic ground than they normally can at halftime, but they have to be mindful of not dispensing more information than can be absorbed, and careful not to allow too much anxiety or, worse, boredom to set in.

Players follow their usual halftime routine. They head for their dressing cubicle to sit and catch their breath. They grab an orange or two and a cold bottle of water or a sports drink. There is plenty of time for a restroom stop, a visit to the trainer's quarters and equipment repair. Walsh insisted

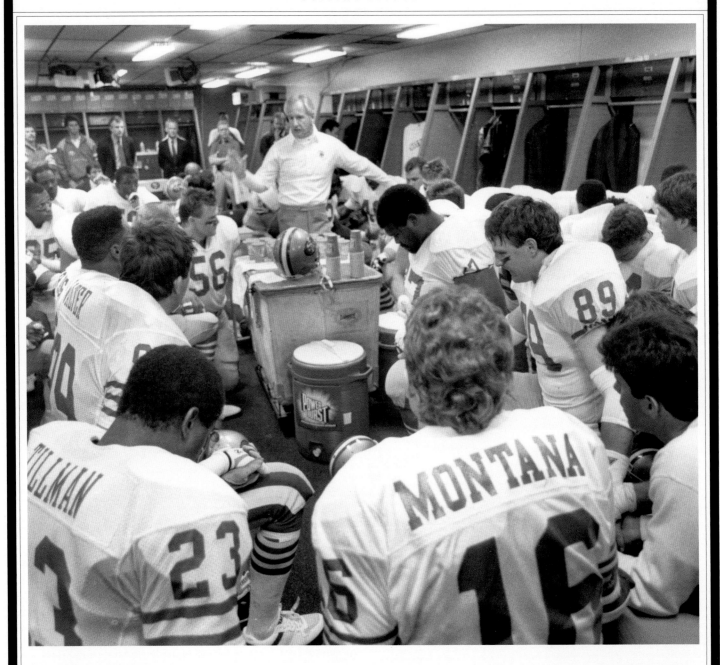

that his players take about 10 minutes to relax before being subjected to a barrage of coaching points.

The assistant coaches who are stationed in the press box head for the locker room before the end of the first half. As soon as they arrive, they illustrate various offensive and defensive schemes by the opponent on display boards in the middle of the room. The illustrations are complemented with photographs showing how plays developed.

The players are divided by units—offense on one side, defense on the other—and the locker room becomes a classroom. The head coach and coordinators talk about what the team did in the first half, how the opponent attacked, and adjustments for the final two quarters.

After that, players gather with their position coaches for more detailed sessions.

Some coaching points that have been made during Super Bowl halftimes are worth noting:

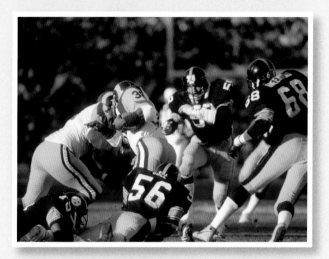

XIV Trailing the Los Angeles Rams, 13-10, the Steelers were unhappy with the performance of their vaunted defense, even though it had allowed only one touchdown and two field goals. "How can you mess up this way?" assistant coach Woody Widenhofer implored of the defensive unit. "Didn't we go over these things a dozen times? You guys are standing out there like statues." The Steelers gave up six more points on the way to a 31-19 victory, their fourth triumph in as many Super Bowls.

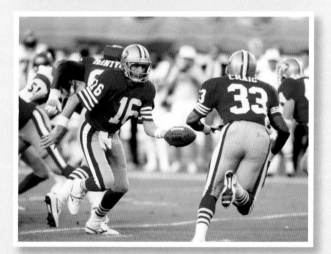

XXIII Tied with the Bengals, 3-3, Bill Walsh and the 49ers offensive coaches determined that their biggest obstacle was Bengals safety David Fulcher. The solution: Use two tight ends to reduce the effectiveness of Fulcher's blitzing and run away from him. The outcome: A 20-16 San Francisco victory decided by Joe Montana's stirring 92-yard touchdown drive in the final 3:10.

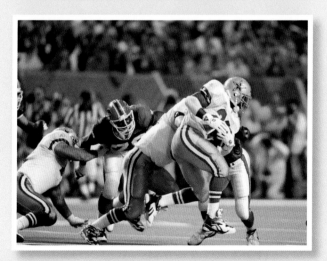

XXVIII Trailing the Bills, 13-6, the Cowboys knew they had to make adjustments on offense. "Get me the ball!" Emmitt Smith shouted at offensive coordinator Norv Turner. Smith had rushed for 41 yards in the first half. Turner later acknowledged that in an effort to establish run-pass balance with his play calling, he had been "forcing some passes that really weren't there." Smith finished with 132 rushing yards and was selected the game's MVP in Dallas' 30-13 victory.

Once the players have been briefed on Xs and Os, the head coach will address the entire squad, usually to establish a theme for the second half. For instance, with his Redskins trailing the Dolphins, 17-10, in Super Bowl XVII, Gibbs reminded his players that they had rallied from larger deficits and that he was certain they would again. Washington won, 27-17.

Baltimore Ravens coach Brian Billick, loquacious by nature, was surprisingly brief after his team built a 10-0 halftime lead over the Giants in Super Bowl XXXV: "If we don't turn the ball over, we're world champs." The Ravens didn't, and rolled to a 34-7 triumph.

Super Bowl procedure calls for the referee to alert both teams three minutes before they are due on the field for the second half. The alert has been premature on occasion. Players charged down the tunnel, only to be held back until the halftime show participants and equipment were cleared from the field. Walsh assigned the 49ers support staff to verify when the time was right to leave the locker room. The last thing players want after a lengthy halftime in the biggest game is to hurry up and then have to wait.

"Either you're sequestered or you're on the field," Walsh says. "You don't want to run a team through a crew that's moving a big stage or have them standing around while the fireworks are still coming down."

"Our profile was always very simple: play sound defense;
win the field position battle; win the time of possession; don't make the big, egregious mistake.
A little conservative for my liking, but that was the formula we had won with leading up to the
Super Bowl, and there was no reason to change. We did take the mentality that we were
going to be more aggressive offensively and take more shots down the field, which we did.
We wanted to get them back on their heels. We felt if we could get up by 10, and let
our defense play to their strengths, that we could control the game."

BRIAN BILLICK, *coach, Ravens*

Coaches who win the Super Bowl have the same thing in common with coaches who win any game: great preparation.

There might not have been a team more ready to dominate a game than the Tampa Bay Buccaneers were before they crushed the Raiders, 48-21, in XXXVII. Buccaneers coach Jon Gruden not only knew what his team had to do to win, but also how to attack the Raiders, whom he had coached the previous season.

As architect of a Raiders offense that was using a good bit of the playbook he himself had authored, Gruden had valuable knowledge to share with the Bucs defense, which ranked No. 1 in the NFL that season. On the plane ride to San Diego for the game, he met with defensive coordinator Monte Kiffin to discuss some of the pass patterns that he anticipated the Raiders would run, as well as their offensive buzzwords and code words.

Gruden had plenty of inside information on Oakland quarterback and league MVP Rich Gannon, right down to how his snap count would sound. Gruden did his best imitation of Gannon during practice, stepping in at quarterback (a position he played at the University of Dayton) on Tampa Bay's scout team offense.

Sure enough, the Bucs defense made Gannon and the NFL's top-ranked offense look inept. Gannon, who had thrown only ten interceptions during the regular season,

Tampa Bay coach Jon Gruden had intimate knowledge of the Oakland Raiders, his team's Super Bowl XXXVII opponent.

had five in the Super Bowl, including three that were returned for touchdowns. He finished with a passer rating of 48.9—his season mark was 97.3.

At times it seemed that the headsets of Gruden and his assistant coaches were plugged into the Raiders' communication system. Both Tampa Bay's offense and defense showed remarkable anticipation. Bucs safety John Lynch, who wore a wireless microphone for television, said on the sideline late in the first half, "Every play they've run, we've run in practice."

Thorough preparation is also a hallmark of Belichick's Super Bowl teams. "He is somewhat of a mad scientist," Patriots safety Rodney Harrison says. "He definitely is the smartest coach I've been around. There is not one detail he overlooks."

"Bill watches every inch of tape," says Pepper Johnson, New England's defensive line coach. "He doesn't just say, 'We have to have a big game on special teams,' and walk out of the room. He says, 'This is who we need to block. This guy has speed. This guy makes tackles.' "

Preparation was also tantamount in Shanahan's mind before Denver's second Super Bowl victory in as many years. "There were people who actually expressed some concern when we had to wear our white uniforms for Super Bowl XXXIII against Atlanta," Shanahan wrote in his book, *Think Like A Champion*.

"But we were so prepared that if we had played in our pajamas, we still would have felt good about our chances."

Mike Shanahan and John Elway celebrated after both Super Bowl XXXII and XXXIII, the final two years of Elway's brilliant 16-year career.

Bill Walsh, on RETIREMENT

"I had known for some weeks that I'd be retiring after the Super Bowl.

No one knew it. I didn't want to distract the squad with it. I didn't want them to 'Play one for Walsh,' or to be thinking about it—they were there to focus on the world championship. The most dramatic moment for me was prior to the game, walking around on the field in Miami, looking at the crowd, all by myself. To be honest with you, I broke down some. I was thinking this was it for me, and it was for the world championship, and I had so much pride to have gotten our team to that point. I thought about the fellowship, the fraternal aspect of it, the bonding with other players and coaches—it had meant an awful lot to me.

As the *Star-Spangled Banner* played before the game, if anybody had watched me, I was on the verge of breaking down. But once it was over, I had a job to do. I had to pull back on my emotions, and totally focus my concentration on winning that game. And, of course, it was one of the great games of all time, our having to pull it out in the last three minutes with a 92-yard drive. It was a game never to be forgotten, and the end of a career that I was so fortunate to have lived."

SIMMS

Great success stories in the Super Bowl are about coaches who are not afraid to take a chance, to do something differently, to do whatever it takes to give their team the best opportunity to win.

I know that might sound simple, but it's not always the case. A lot of coaches take the safe route because they worry about being second-guessed—and they should. If you take a chance and lose, even though you were in the Super Bowl, you've stuck one foot out the door on your way to being fired. If you win, you go down in history as a genius.

It takes courage. Some of the best coaches and strongest people in the world don't have that kind of courage.

The earliest example I can think of in the Super Bowl goes all the way back to Vince Lombardi. I heard a story about how, as the Packers were getting ready to play the Kansas City Chiefs in the first Super Bowl, Lombardi was looking at film of Kansas City's defense, and he said, "I don't like playing this team because we can't run the football well against them. I think we're going to have to throw the ball to win."

Lombardi kept looking at film, trying to figure out a way to run the football because that was what he wanted to do. The "Green Bay Sweep" was what the Packers were about and what had made him famous. But when Lombardi realized the Packers were better off passing, he said, "Bart Starr, win the game by throwing." And he did. Starr threw for 250 yards and two touchdowns to lead Green Bay to a 35–10 victory.

If the Packers had lost, the legacy of Lombardi might not be what it is.

We'd be saying, "Ah, he really blew that one. He tried to run that 'Green Bay Sweep,' and it cost him the Super Bowl."

The week before the New York Giants faced the Denver Broncos in Super Bowl XXI, our coach, Bill Parcells, set the tone for what would be a very aggressive approach by our team. He kept telling me, "Don't be afraid to take chances." I can still remember the look on his face. Even if, deep down inside, he was as fearful as anyone of losing in the Super Bowl, he didn't show it. And he remained that way after the opening kickoff.

In the second half, we were trailing 10–9 and facing a fourth-and-1. What do we do? We go for it, and it leads to a touchdown. We even ran a flea-flicker to set up another score. We were taking chances, doing risky things, and we ended up with a 39–20 victory.

I look at Parcells' coaching job against the Buffalo Bills in Super Bowl XXV as another example of successful risk-taking. Without question, the Bills were the more talented team. But the Giants were patient. They kept running the football, eating the time up. They kept taking advantage of the aggressive players on Buffalo's defense with tiny boot passes. On each completion, there were just enough yards to get a first down. Three more plays and more time off the clock.

The Bills had that explosive no-huddle offense, and the Giants' methodical offensive strategy slowed them down. It was a well-orchestrated team concept that—along with Scott Norwood's missed field goal at the end—allowed the Giants to win the game, 20-19.

Bill Belichick took one of the all-time coaching risks when he led the New England Patriots against the St. Louis Rams in Super Bowl XXXVI. And he did it by keeping his team's risks on defense to a minimum. When the Patriots played

the Rams in Foxboro that season, they blitzed Kurt Warner like crazy, which made sense, considering Belichick's creative blitz schemes and that he was going against a pocket passer in an offense that liked to throw the ball. But when the Patriots played the Rams in the Super Bowl, Belichick reversed his field 180 degrees. His defense was conservative and physical, and that had as much to do with the Patriots' 20-17 win as Tom Brady's MVP performance or Adam Vinatieri's last-second field goal.

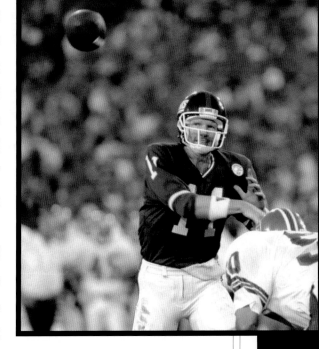

As the game began, it didn't even cross my mind that Belichick might go that route, but it sure made sense as I watched it. Throw off the rhythm of the quarterback; make him hold the ball just a little bit longer. Warner's not quite as effective a thrower when you make him hold it. The less aggressive approach gives your defense a little bit more time to hit the quarterback, so you get more hits. And no matter who you are, when the hits start piling up on you, your decision-making suffers. The Patriots scored a touchdown on a pass interception in that game, too.

It's the same in any business: Sometimes you've got to take a little bit of a chance to go along with all your studying and all your knowledge. A little bit of risk-taking often can make something great. That would hold true for coaches in the Super Bowl.

Dominance
by Decade

60s 70s 80s 90s 00s

The New England Patriots' third Super Bowl victory in four years and second in a row, achieved in February 2005, validated the organization as an NFL dynasty. It placed the Patriots in the company of the Green Bay Packers of the 1960s, the Pittsburgh Steelers of the 1970s, the San Francisco 49ers of the 1980s and the Dallas Cowboys of the 1990s.

The Patriots of 2001-2004 are not on the fringe of this elite group. Depending on the point of view, they could well be at the top of the list. Unlike the others, their success came in an era when keeping a great team together had proven to be nearly impossible, and the NFL had never been more competitive.

Don Shula, who coached the 1972 and 1973 Miami Dolphins to Super Bowl victories—the '72 squad was the only unbeaten team in NFL history—marvels at how Patriots coach Bill Belichick handled the difficult task of managing his team's payroll to stay under the salary cap while retaining most of his key players. The salary cap and free agency provide players the opportunities to change teams, and top players in the prime of their careers are

always in demand. The teams they leave usually replace them with younger and less expensive talent. To succeed, coaches must be highly proficient at preparing inexperienced players to make an immediate positive impact.

Shula, who retired in 1996 with more victories than any other coach in NFL history, says that in his final few seasons he spent more time in salary cap meetings than he had ever previously spent in finance-related sessions. He increasingly found himself making decisions based more on cap-dollar ramifications than on football.

"That was a little hard to get used to," Shula says. "But now everybody has to get used to that. The thing you want to do now is figure out how to work with the cap because there's always somebody that figures it out. Obviously Belichick figured it out."

Equally amazing is that Belichick got a majority of his players to accept a philosophy he constantly preaches: The greater good of the team is more important than individual glory. The Patriots are so humble that

SIXTEEN PLAYERS APPEARED IN ALL THREE SUPER BOWLS WON BY THE NEW ENGLAND PATRIOTS FOLLOWING THE 2001, 2003 AND 2004 SEASONS. THOSE PLAYERS AND THE NUMBER OF TIMES THEY HAD A STARTING ROLE:

OFFENSE

T	MATT LIGHT (3)
G	JOE ANDRUZZI (3)
QB	TOM BRADY (3)
K	ADAM VINATIERI (3)
WR	TROY BROWN (2)
FB	PATRICK PASS (1)
G-C	MATT CHATMAN
RB	KEVIN FAULK

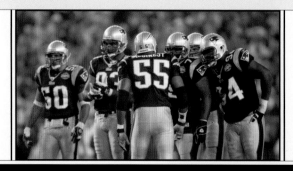

DEFENSE

LB	MIKE VRABEL (3)
LB	TEDY BRUSCHI (3)
LB	ROMAN PHIFER (3)
T	RICHARD SEYMOUR (2)
LB	WILLIE McGINEST (2)
DB	JE'ROD CHERRY
LB	LARRY IZZO
LB	TED JOHNSON

their players and coaches avoid any hint of making dynasty declarations, or addressing the subject whatsoever. "Other people can talk about it," linebacker Tedy Bruschi says, knowing that many will gladly oblige.

The Patriots' 24-21 victory over the Philadelphia Eagles in Super Bowl XXXIX was typical of many of their wins. Quarterback Tom Brady, MVP of the Pats' previous Super Bowl triumphs and perhaps their only player who had attained superstar status, was an important factor in beating the Eagles—but he wasn't the MVP. That honor belonged to Deion Branch, who caught 11 passes for 133 yards. Impressive numbers, although, like almost every other Patriots victory during their championship era, this one wasn't

about big numbers or glitz. It was about a workmanlike effort by a club that had been the NFL's consummate team.

These Patriots teams had been a collection of role players, with someone different apt to make a game-turning big play in any given situation. The roster included players capable of performing effectively at several positions. When starting cornerbacks Ty Law and Tyrone Poole suffered injuries during the 2004 season, wide receiver Troy Brown moved to defensive back and made three interceptions. In each of the last two Super Bowls, linebacker Mike Vrabel caught a touchdown pass as a tight end.

Fielding a group of players willing to do whatever was best

"Everybody knows Tom Brady is a proven winner.

He may not put up the big 5,000 passing yards in a season, and all that stuff. But he's thrown for 30 touchdowns in a season. The guy's just amazing. The most important thing is: Can you put your team in the end zone? And can you get the wins for your team? He's proven that he's the master at putting up wins.

Tom's got that whole California, laid-back, surfer-type dude thing going. He never shows any signs of being shook-up in big situations. Normally a guy under that kind of pressure, you're gonna make some mistakes. But Tom's been pretty much flawless in our Super Bowls. He does a great job of staying calm, and a great job of making the right reads under pressure, and avoiding pressure when its coming at him.

That's why he's the first player to win two Super Bowl MVPs at such a young age."

TROY BROWN, *wide receiver, Patriots*

for the team, at the expense of personal glory and inflated statistics, contributed to a perception that the Patriots were not as talented as previous dynasties. That perhaps made their championship reign more impressive than that of some other teams.

Comparisons are made between the Patriots and the Packers teams that won five NFL championships in seven years during the 1960s, in particular the Green Bay teams that won the first two Super Bowls, in 1966 and 1967. It is hardly a stretch to put Belichick in the same company as Vince Lombardi, coach of those Packers teams. New England's Super Bowl XXXIX triumph pushed Belichick's

postseason record to 10-1, better than that of Lombardi or any other coach in NFL history. But there is more to the Belichick-Lombardi parallel than numbers. Both received the lion's share of credit for their teams' success because it arguably had as much, if not more, to do with their coaching as with their players' skills and performance.

Belichick and his assistants designed and implemented strategy that maximized the production of athletes who might not have even been on the field, let alone attained Super Bowl glory, had they been playing in another system for another coaching staff.

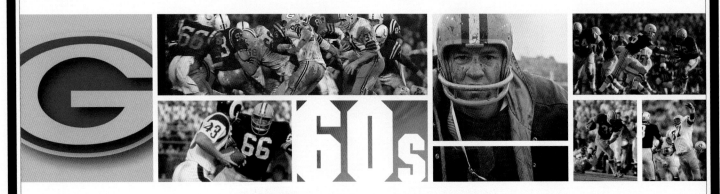

In 1959 Lombardi became coach of a Packers team that had gone 1-10-1 and yielded an NFL-high 32 points a game the previous season. Two years later, despite no major changes to the roster, he led Green Bay to the first of its five titles of that era. Bart Starr, Paul Hornung, Ray Nitschke, Jim Taylor and others became legendary players, but by the mid-1960s the Packers were an aging squad that relied more on savvy and experience than on physical skills. Lombardi, with his considerable leadership skills and coaching expertise, managed to drain what was left in his championship nucleus, leading the Packers to convincing victories in the first two Super Bowls, over the Kansas City Chiefs and the Oakland Raiders.

Although he was proud of the Packers' first three titles, Lombardi was especially pleased with their 35-10 victory in Super Bowl I following the 1966 season. With a chance to not only prove the Packers' supremacy to the rest of the football world, but also the established NFL's superiority over the upstart American Football League, he approached the game as if it would define his legacy. Asked why he placed such significance on Super Bowl I, Lombardi replied, "It is important because it has never been played before. It is a first game, and that in itself makes it important to me and the team."

The Chiefs made a game of it for a half. With Green Bay holding a four-point lead in the third quarter, the Packers'

"Bart Starr was as accurate up to 40 yards as any quarterback in NFL history—period. There's an erroneous opinion among some fans that if you can throw the football 60 and 70 yards, you should be a great quarterback. Bart did not have the strongest of arms. He didn't have an arm like Norm Van Brocklin did, for heaven's sakes. Ed Brown of the Chicago Bears could throw it 95 yards, but would you want Ed Brown as your quarterback or would you want Bart Starr? I played with Bart for nine years, and I'll guarantee you he never made 10 mental mistakes the whole time."

PAUL HORNUNG, *running back, Packers*

Familiar Faces

The Green Bay Packers had the same starters in Super Bowl I and II at all but center and both running back positions. In fact, 12 of the team's 22 starters remained the same from 1961 to 1967, when Green Bay won five championships. The regulars on all five title teams:

OFFENSE		DEFENSE	
G	Jerry Kramer	T	Henry Jordan
G	Fuzzy Thurston	T	Ron Kostelnik
T	Forrest Gregg	E	Willie Davis
T	Bob Skoronski	LB	Ray Nitschke
WR	Boyd Dowler	CB	Herb Adderley
QB	Bart Starr	FS	Willie Wood

Paul Hornung, on EGOS

"You can't have a Hornung and a Taylor in the same backfield in today's game.
Dallas tried it with Herschel Walker and Tony Dorsett, and as great as they were, you couldn't put them on the same team. But we could put Hornung and Taylor together because I wasn't jealous of Jimmy Taylor whatsoever. Bart Starr wasn't jealous of me, and I wasn't jealous of Bart Starr. There were three Hall of Famers in the same backfield, and we got along. I knew what my job was. Jimmy knew what his job was, and Bart knew what his job was. We did our jobs—that's the way it's supposed to be."

Willie Wood intercepted a Len Dawson pass and returned it 50 yards to the Kansas City 5. Green Bay scored on the next play, and the Chiefs were deflated.

The following year the Packers scored a last-second, 21-17 victory over Dallas for the NFL championship in one of the most memorable games in football history. Played in subzero temperatures on the "frozen tundra" of Green Bay's Lambeau Field, the "Ice Bowl" provided unforgettable drama. The Packers gained possession at their 32-yard line with 5:04 to play and the Cowboys leading, 17-14. With 16 seconds remaining and the Packers two feet from the goal line, Lombardi could have played it safe and had Starr try to pass into the end zone. If no one was open, Starr could have thrown the ball out of bounds, and the Packers would have had time for a field goal that could have tied the score and sent the game into overtime. Instead, at Starr's urging, Lombardi called for a quarterback sneak. Starr followed guard Jerry Kramer into the end zone for the game-winning touchdown.

In the days prior to Super Bowl II, rumors swirled that the game would be Lombardi's last as the Packers' coach, which proved to be the case. At halftime, with the Packers holding a 16-7 lead over the Raiders, Kramer waited for Lombardi to leave the locker room before delivering a message to his teammates: "Let's win this one for the old man!" The Packers proceeded to roll to a 33-14 triumph.

The Steelers of the 1970s remain a lasting symbol of sustained excellence, the first team to win the Super Bowl four times. The Dolphins and Cowboys might have been prominent in that decade—each won the Super Bowl twice—but their accomplishments paled in comparison with the accomplishments of the Steelers, champions after the 1974, 1975, 1978 and 1979 seasons.

"What it all comes down to in deciding which team was the best," Don Shula says, "is how many Super Bowls you won. That's the truest measure."

Just how dominant those Steelers teams were became even more apparent in subsequent years. Nine Steelers of that era, in addition to coach Chuck Noll and owners Art and Dan Rooney, were elected to the Pro Football Hall of Fame.

It was an incredible run of success, forged by the deft but gentle hand of cigar-chomping owner Art Rooney Sr. What made the Steelers so good was that they consistently performed at a high level and never took the proverbial day off against a lesser opponent. Consider that from 1972 to 1979—an eight-year stretch in which they made the playoffs every season

Art Rooney's Pittsburgh Steelers were a woebegone team until he hired Chuck Noll, who set a championship course in the 1970s.

"Joe Greene was kind of the Steelers' spokesperson.

There were many times after a football game that I wasn't really sure why we lost or why we won. I waited to read in the newspaper Monday what Joe had to say about it, so I could understand what happened. There was a lot of respect for Joe as a player and as a person. He was a great football player."

In Their Words

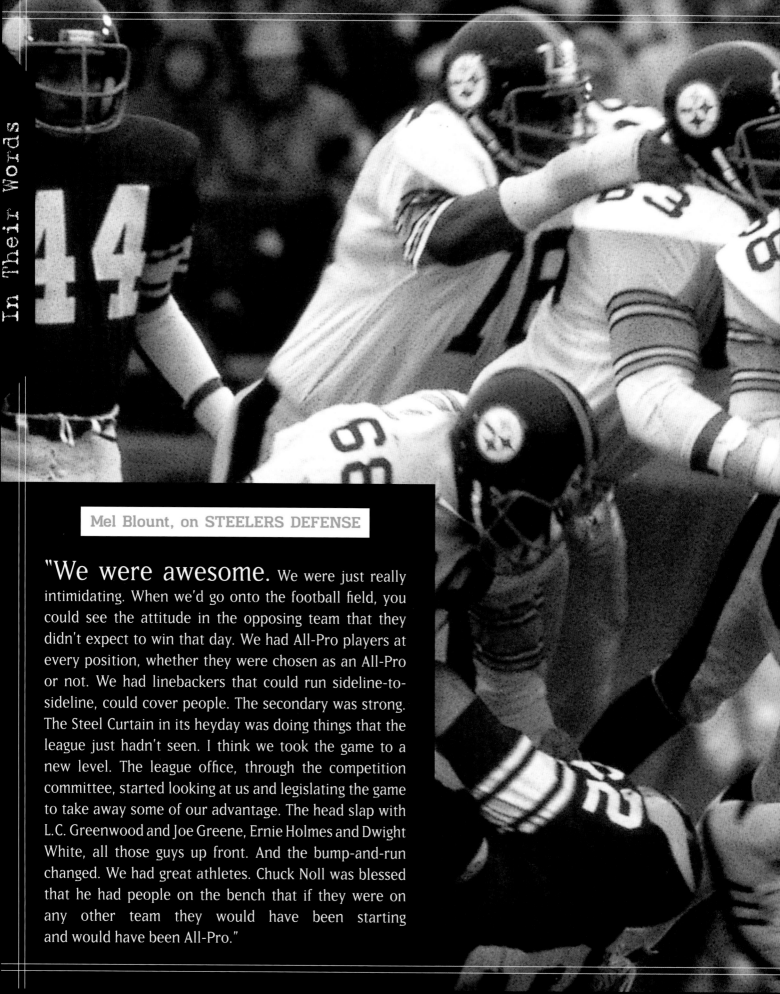

Mel Blount, on STEELERS DEFENSE

"We were awesome. We were just really intimidating. When we'd go onto the football field, you could see the attitude in the opposing team that they didn't expect to win that day. We had All-Pro players at every position, whether they were chosen as an All-Pro or not. We had linebackers that could run sideline-to-sideline, could cover people. The secondary was strong. The Steel Curtain in its heyday was doing things that the league just hadn't seen. I think we took the game to a new level. The league office, through the competition committee, started looking at us and legislating the game to take away some of our advantage. The head slap with L.C. Greenwood and Joe Greene, Ernie Holmes and Dwight White, all those guys up front. And the bump-and-run changed. We had great athletes. Chuck Noll was blessed that he had people on the bench that if they were on any other team they would have been starting and would have been All-Pro."

TERRY BRADSHAW

FRANCO HARRIS

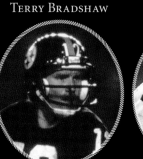

LYNN SWANN

JOHN STALLWORTH

and won four Super Bowls—the Steelers' record against opponents that had a losing record was 50-1.

"What we had was an undeniable hatred of losing," says Terry Bradshaw, the quarterback of those teams, twice the Super Bowl MVP and a member of the Hall of Fame. "We laughed and giggled and had fun playing, but we had the fangs and the blood and slobber, too."

Before they became wildly successful, the Steelers endured years of failure and embarrassment. Unable to muster the finances to operate on their own, they once merged with the Eagles for a season and the Cardinals for

the next. They made the playoffs for the first time in 1948, but shortly after that season their coach, Jock Sutherland, unexpectedly dropped dead. In the 1950s, quarterbacks Sid Luckman, John Unitas, Len Dawson and Jack Kemp slipped through the Steelers' fingers. In 1964, they obtained second- and fourth-round draft choices from the Bears in exchange for their 1965 first-round choice. The Steelers chose forgettable players named James Kelly and Ben McGee. The Bears used their pick from Pittsburgh to draft Dick Butkus.

The Steelers' fortunes began to change in 1969. The

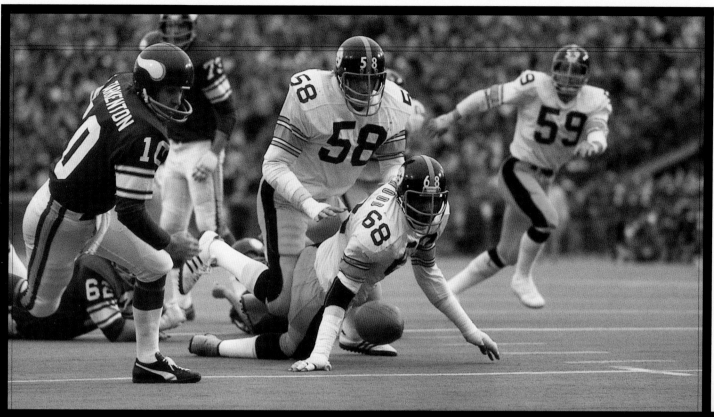

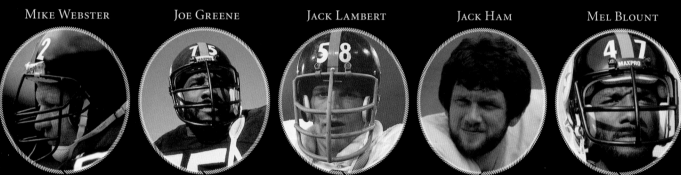

MIKE WEBSTER   JOE GREENE   JACK LAMBERT   JACK HAM   MEL BLOUNT

biggest development that year was the arrival of defensive tackle Joe Greene, a player who would define the position over the next decade. Bradshaw, with his strong arm and exceptional playmaking ability, came a year later as the No. 1 overall pick of the draft. The Steelers won a coin flip with the Bears—both had a 1-13 record in 1969—to determine who would draft first in 1970. Steelers president Dan Rooney, Art's son, represented Pittsburgh at the coin flip ceremony in a New Orleans hotel. Dan let Bears vice president Ed McCaskey call the flip of a 1921 silver dollar by NFL commissioner Pete Rozelle. McCaskey called heads,

and the coin landed tails. Rozelle gave the coin to Rooney, who turned it over to Noll at dinner that evening and told the coach it was a "sign of good things to come."

Indeed it was. Franco Harris joined Rocky Bleier in the Steelers backfield in 1972. Then came Pittsburgh's incredible 1974 draft that yielded four future Hall of Fame players: wide receivers Lynn Swann and John Stallworth, linebacker Jack Lambert and center Mike Webster. Swann and Stallworth were backups as rookies, but soon became a remarkable tandem that was a perfect fit for Bradshaw's bombs-away style.

The Pittsburgh Steelers' 1974 draft class is widely regarded as the best in NFL history. Of the 21 drafted, nine played in the NFL, and four are in the Hall of Fame. A list of those who played in the NFL:

Rd.	No.	Player	Comment
1	21	Lynn Swann, wr, Southern Cal	Hall of Fame
2	46	Jack Lambert, lb, Kent State	Hall of Fame
4	82	John Stallworth, wr, Alabama A&M	Hall of Fame
4	100	Jimmy Allen, db, UCLA	8 seasons, 4 with Steelers
5	125	Mike Webster, c, Wisconsin	Hall of Fame
6	149	James Wolf, de, Prairie View A&M	2 seasons, 1 with Steelers
6	150	Rick Druschel, g, North Carolina State	1 season with Steelers
9	223	Tommy Reamon, rb, Missouri	1 season with Kansas City
9	229	Charlie Davis, ot, Texas Christian	7 seasons, 1 with Steelers

Lambert brought tremendous toughness and intimidation to the defense. Considered too small by some teams, he won over the Steelers when their scouts assigned to track him at Kent State watched him dive at a teammate during a parking-lot practice, and nonchalantly get up and pick cinders out of his bleeding face. Before Pittsburgh's 21-17 victory over Dallas in Super Bowl X in Miami, Lambert told a reporter that he hoped a shark would bite off one of Roger Staubach's arms.

Perhaps the most impressive measure of the Steelers' greatness came in Super Bowl XIII against Dallas. The Steelers had the AFC's ninth-ranked running game; the Cowboys' defense was first in the NFL at stopping the run. Pittsburgh managed only two first downs rushing. Rather than challenge the Cowboys' strength, the Steelers relied on another facet of their remarkable team. Bradshaw passed for 318 yards and four touchdowns in a 35-31 victory.

The performance was a classic example of Noll's persistent mantra: "Whatever it takes." Ray Mansfield, the starting center on Pittsburgh's first two Super Bowl teams, says, "We heard that so often, we always

said he had it embroidered on his shorts."

The most entertaining of the Steelers' Super Bowl victories was the final one, a 31-19 win over the Los Angeles Rams. The lead changed sides seven times. The game turned on two plays in the fourth quarter. Bradshaw, facing third-and-8 at the Steelers 27, hooked up with Stallworth on a deep post pattern for a 73-yard touchdown that put Pittsburgh in front, 24-19. The second key play was Lambert's interception of a Vince Ferragamo pass deep in Steelers' territory.

In the locker room after that game, Super Bowl XIV, Greene offered a battle cry for the following season: "One for the thumb in '81." But most of the Steelers, whether they would admit it or not, had to know that their remarkable run was near an end, if not over. The team was aging and skills were eroding, and no future Hall of Fame players were on the horizon to take over for those that had been in place for a decade. As the Steelers' greatness faded, a team out West was ready for its run of glory.

"When you look at us against the Dallas Cowboys, it was a rivalry of image and style. The country looked at us as being a physical, brutish, blue-collar football team. The country viewed the Cowboys as a finesse, stylish, intelligent football team. We resented—and still resent—that anyone referred to the Cowboys as 'America's Team.' You know what America's Team is? A team that wins the Super Bowl, that's America's Team. That was us, four times."

LYNN SWANN, *wide receiver, Steelers*

Harris Barton, on ROGER CRAIG

"Blocking for Roger Craig is a chance to feel real good about yourself, especially on the plays that you know he likes to run. He likes to run that outside sweep, and he likes to run the counter. When you hear those plays called, you want to block hard for him because you know Roger Craig. If you get him into the secondary, he's going to make things happen.

He's taken some severe hits, and I've seen him come back and just continue to run and run. He's just one of the hardest workers I've ever met. Everybody tries to say they're like Roger Craig, but until you get out there and run like he does, then I'm not a believer."

The San Francisco 49ers took control of the 1980s by becoming the next four-time Super Bowl winner. Like the Steelers, the 49ers had experienced lean times. They were 2-14 in both 1978 and 1979 before Bill Walsh came along and guided them to a conference championship in 1981.

The Steelers offense had tested and pressured a defense's deep coverage. Now came the 49ers offense to test a defense's patience. Walsh's West Coast offense was based on precise timing and passes delivered with a gentle rhythm rather than rifle-like velocity. The attack was more horizontal than vertical, but every bit as effective as any offense ever introduced into the NFL.

Walsh found the ideal quarterback to run his scheme in the 1979 draft: third-round selection Joe Montana. "Joe's comprehension and mastery of the system was the key," says Walsh, who coached the 49ers to their first three Super Bowl victories and then turned the team over to George Seifert, who guided the 49ers to their fourth championship in the 1980s (and a fifth in the '90s). "Joe understood exactly what had to be done in a given situation, and he adjusted if things broke down."

THE SAN FRANCISCO 49ERS WON THE SUPER BOWL FOUR TIMES IN THE NINE-YEAR SPAN FROM 1981 TO 1989. FIVE PLAYERS APPEARED IN ALL FOUR GAMES, AND FIVE OTHERS APPEARED IN THREE OF THE FOUR GAMES. THE FIVE WHO APPEARED IN ALL FOUR—ALL EXCEPT WILSON HAD STARTING ROLES IN EACH GAME:

QB JOE MONTANA   CB ERIC WRIGHT   LB KEENA TURNER   WR MIKE WILSON   CB-S RONNIE LOTT

THE OTHER FIVE WHO APPEARED IN THREE OF THE FOUR GAMES AND THE NUMBER OF TIMES THEY HAD A STARTING ROLE:

G-C RANDY CROSS (3)   OG GUY MCINTYRE (2)   RB ROGER CRAIG (3)   OT BUBBA PARIS (2)   NT MICHAEL CARTER (2)

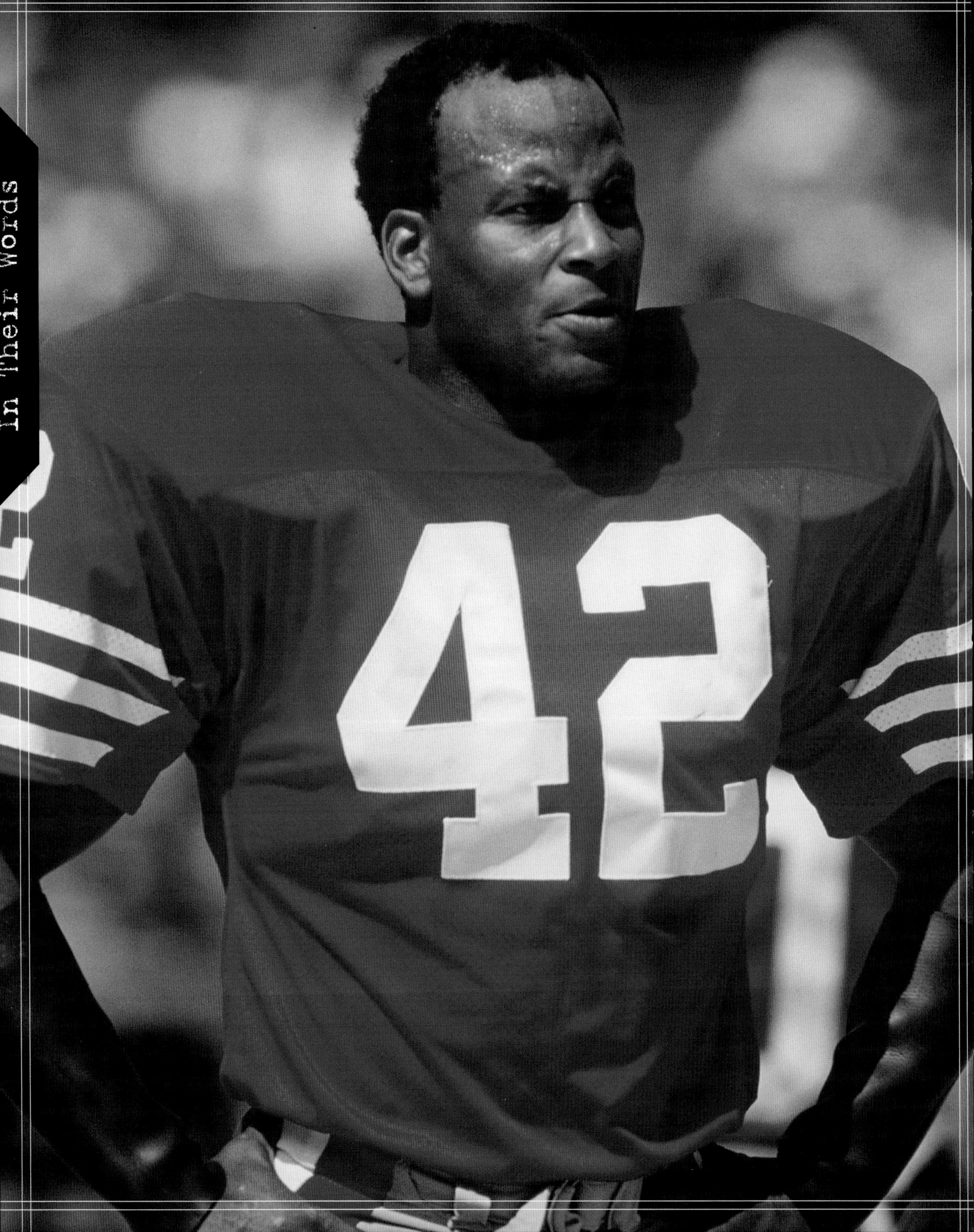
42

"When you're building an organization, you want guys that want to achieve and can lift other people up. Somehow grab another guy and say 'Hey, we can get better.' That was Joe Montana, Jerry Rice, Dwight Clark, Hacksaw Reynolds, Fred Dean, Eric Wright, Carlton Williamson, Dwight Hicks and a lot more of us. Everybody in that group in their own way were overachievers, yet didn't need to stand out in front and say, 'Hey, look, I'm the guy.' To have all those great athletes around one another and come together and believe that the only way we can get this done is to do it together and really compete against ourselves, but also while we're competing against ourselves, make sure we lift one another up—that's a very special group. We had a lot of people that were great achievers. But in their own mind, they were always pessimistic, kind of saying, 'Well, maybe I can't do it. Maybe I can't do it.' Having that mind-set allowed them to constantly push themselves."

Quite often, the 49ers passing game also served the same purpose as a running attack, with Montana completing short, safe throws underneath the coverage. Big plays generally came when one of his receivers, Jerry Rice and John Taylor, broke free for long gains after the catch. Not that the 49ers couldn't run the ball. They might not have done it with much power, but they were effective, using high-stepping Roger Craig on traps and counters.

The 49ers also had an exceptional defense, led by cornerback/safety Ronnie Lott. On the way to their convincing victory over Miami and record-setting quarterback Dan Marino in Super Bowl XIX, the 49ers allowed a league-low 14.2 points a game during the 1984 regular season.

Part of San Francisco's success was due to its remarkable

ability to win on the road. From 1981 to 1989 the 49ers had a better road record than the home records of every other NFL team. Some of that could be credited to the care afforded the team by 49ers management on road trips. Each player had two seats on the team's chartered flights, aiding their comfort and stoking their pride. Most also had a hotel room to themselves rather than having to share with a teammate, which was the practice of most teams.

Winning on the road was a major theme of Walsh's addresses to the squad. "He talked about how it was us against the entire city, about how tough we had to be, about what a thrill it would be to take that win away from that team in its home stadium," says Randy Cross, a starting offensive lineman on three of those Super Bowl teams.

Jerry Rice, on JOE MONTANA

"My fondest memory of Joe?

Super Bowl XXIII, the final drive, I'll never forget it. Just the way he ran onto the football field, came into the huddle, didn't say anything, just dropped down on one knee and called the play, I just knew inside that we would win that football game. Just because of his presence."

The 1990s belonged to the Dallas Cowboys. When Jerry Jones bought the franchise in 1989, the team was a mere shell of what it had been in the glory days of the 1970s.

Jones hired brash Jimmy Johnson to replace stoic Tom Landry as coach. Johnson quickly set the course to rebuild a franchise that had become known as America's Team when its stars were Roger Staubach, Tony Dorsett, Randy White and Ed "Too Tall" Jones. Johnson assembled a new cast of dynamic playmakers that included Troy Aikman, Emmitt Smith and Michael Irvin. The 1990s Cowboys did something the 1970s Dallas teams never accomplished: three Super Bowl victories in a four-year span. Johnson coached the first two

championship teams, and Barry Switzer the third.

Aikman, Smith and Irvin grabbed most of the headlines, but the Dallas defense played a large role in all three championship games. In Super Bowl XXVII against the Buffalo Bills, the Cowboys forced a record nine turnovers. A year later, in a rematch with the Bills, Leon Lett forced a fumble that James Washington returned 46 yards for the game-tying touchdown in what turned out to be a 30-13 triumph.

In Super Bowl XXX, Larry Brown earned MVP honors by twice intercepting Neil O'Donnell in a victory over the Steelers. It marked a record eighth Super Bowl appearance for the Cowboys, and was the fifth championship in the franchise's history.

ELEVEN PLAYERS MAINTAINED A STARTING POSITION FOR THE DALLAS COWBOYS IN EACH OF THE TEAM'S THREE SUPER BOWL VICTORIES IN THE 1990S, AND ANOTHER EIGHT PLAYERS APPEARED IN ALL THREE GAMES. THE REGULARS ON ALL THREE TITLE TEAMS:

OFFENSE

G	NATE NEWTON
T	MARK TUINEI
T	ERIK WILLIAMS
TE	JAY NOVACEK
WR	MICHAEL IRVIN
RB	EMMITT SMITH
FB	DARYL JOHNSTON
QB	TROY AIKMAN

DEFENSE

E	CHARLES HALEY
E	TONY TOLBERT
CB	LARRY BROWN

The other eight players who appeared in all three games and the number of times they had a starting role:

LB	Robert Jones (2)	LB	Dixon Edwards (1)
DT	Leon Lett (2)	OL	Dale Hellestrae
DE	Russell Maryland (2)	DE	Chad Hennings
LB-S	Darren Woodson (2)	LB	Godfrey Myles

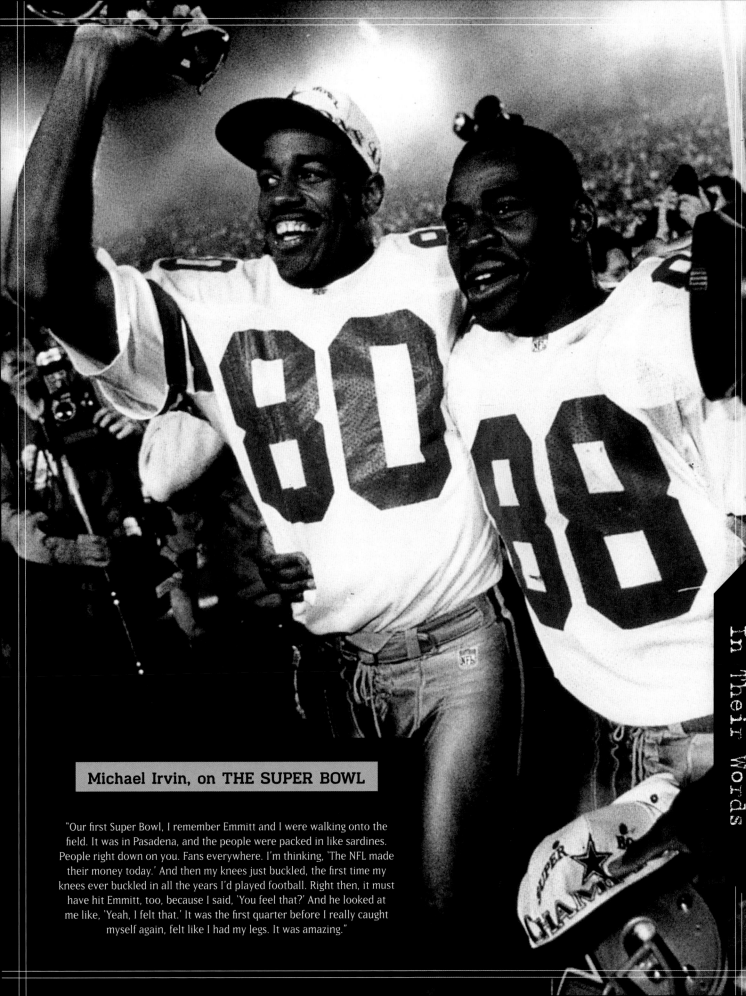

Michael Irvin, on THE SUPER BOWL

"Our first Super Bowl, I remember Emmitt and I were walking onto the field. It was in Pasadena, and the people were packed in like sardines. People right down on you. Fans everywhere. I'm thinking, 'The NFL made their money today.' And then my knees just buckled, the first time my knees ever buckled in all the years I'd played football. Right then, it must have hit Emmitt, too, because I said, 'You feel that?' And he looked at me like, 'Yeah, I felt that.' It was the first quarter before I really caught myself again, felt like I had my legs. It was amazing."

"Right or wrong, quarterbacks are judged on every game. We're judged on everything that we do. That's why I've said, 'Boy, if you're going to get to a Super Bowl, you sure hope you win it.' Because the stigma that goes with losing the Super Bowl is almost worse than having never made it to a Super Bowl. There's tremendous pressure on you not only to perform and play well, but for your team to win. I think about Jim Kelly, for instance. It's unfortunate that he went to four straight Super Bowls and failed to win any of them. People don't know how difficult it was to get to four straight Super Bowls. We all know what's at stake when we go into it. But Jim Kelly and that team haven't gotten the credit they should, and that's disappointing to me."

TROY AIKMAN'S SUPER BOWL
XXVIII RING

Emmitt Smith, on THE COWBOYS

"It's a great feeling to know that you're just that good, that no matter what anybody else does, you're good enough to knock them off. Not only are you good, but your second team is just as good. That's what made our glory years so special: We were so good, we rotated guys in and out and didn't miss a beat. I don't think you can bring up another team in the 1990s to compare with us—we were that dominant, that talented offensively and defensively. We had the whole package. If we got beat, we got beat because the other team played very well and we played very poorly. They were the best team on that particular day, but that's all it was."

BRADSHAW

When you get down to it, it's always about the titles—period. I don't care how many yards you rush for, how many passes you complete. If you didn't win a championship, get out of my way. I don't want to hear about it.

Nobody has ever asked me, "Hey, Terry, how many touchdown passes did you throw?" I don't know. It wasn't very many. But I do know that when I was quarterbacking the Steelers, we won four Super Bowls in six seasons during the 1970s. That made us a dynasty. And I do believe that we had the best of the Super Bowl dynasties, primarily because we had the best defense.

The Cowboys of the 1990s would be a close second because their coach, Jimmy Johnson, was so defense-oriented. They had an explosive offense. They could run it; they could throw it. But they had a truly dominant defense when Jimmy was there. That Dallas team would have been very hard for us to handle. In the prime of both teams, it would have been interesting. It would have been a good game.

The 49ers of the 1980s rank right up there, too. They had a good system, and an excellent coach in Bill Walsh. I'm not saying they couldn't have beaten us, but I don't think their defense was anything near what our Steel Curtain was.

Players from other teams would actually come up to us in the offseason and say, "We knew we were going to lose to you guys. We were scared of the black and gold when they came up to the line of scrimmage." I definitely think that our team matched up well with everybody. We had a very chameleon-like offense—we could run it down your throat, or we could throw it on you.

The Patriots' dynasty—they won three Super Bowls from 2001 to 2004—is extra special because of the challenges they have had to overcome with free agency and the salary cap. I, for one, am sitting in awe of the Patriots. They're a team that you look at and say, "We can beat this team." And then they just go out and beat you.

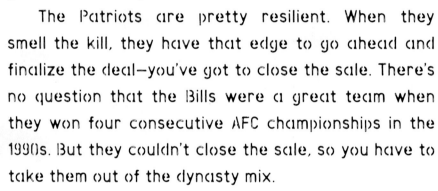

The Patriots are pretty resilient. When they smell the kill, they have that edge to go ahead and finalize the deal—you've got to close the sale. There's no question that the Bills were a great team when they won four consecutive AFC championships in the 1990s. But they couldn't close the sale, so you have to take them out of the dynasty mix.

Most of the NFL dynasties had three main ingredients: A great quarterback (I mean that as a general statement rather than a sign of arrogance), a great defense and depth. We had all the pieces: Lynn Swann, John Stallworth, Franco Harris, Rocky Bleier and Mike Webster, to name a few. With very few exceptions, we did it with the same people. That's what blows me away. And we were very fortunate that our injuries were always very minor, especially to our stars.

We were confident, but that didn't mean we weren't nervous before those Super Bowls. We were. I think the fear of losing is something that's always there with all players, whether they admit it or not.

Once you start playing, you have to understand that the team you're playing is the best from the other conference, so they're very capable of winning the game. You just trust yourself. You don't panic. We had that rare ability to remain calm. We got behind a lot. We'd turn the ball over. We had punts blocked, field goals missed. But we never panicked, and that's another important characteristic of a dynasty team.

For whatever reason, the bigger the game was, the more comfortable I felt. You don't have time to be panicky. You have to execute plays, and you cannot do that if you panic. Your mind won't function. Your brain gets cloudy.

No matter how good we were, nobody knew how hard it was to beat the Browns in Cleveland, or the Oilers in Houston, or the Cowboys in Dallas, or the Raiders in Oakland. In a period of six years, there were numerous challenges to us, and sometimes we failed. But when we won, regardless of the score, we recognized how fortunate we were. Maybe we got the right bounce. Maybe we got the right call. Maybe we had a little bit of a lucky play here and there.

We won the games we were supposed to win. We also fought hard and won most of the games against teams that were our equal. We were pretty resilient.

We always remained focused, totally focused, even when we did face letdown obstacles. Sometimes it was just a little bit hard to get up for certain teams that weren't winning, such as Chicago or maybe Cincinnati. But Chuck Noll, like all the great coaches, was always able to keep us grounded, which is very important.

We had enough great players that were able to squash any talk of dynasty, that didn't talk about how great we were. We were able to keep it low-key. When you're in the middle of a dynasty, the media always tries to bring it to your attention. But as a player, you're sensitive to this kind of talk for fear of losing your edge, so you always brush it off.

Eventually you're able to sit back and evaluate your career. And the conclusion is that you were really good for a period of time and won multiple titles. It's then that you can allow yourself to wear that dynasty tag—with pride.

Grace
Under Pressure

The key to making the
BIG PLAY,
Bill Walsh believes, is approaching it like any other play.

Even if it is the Super Bowl, with millions of people watching and the air so thick with tension that, for most players, taking a deep breath is like trying to suck molasses through a straw. Even if it is likely to be the play that decides a world championship or defines a career, Walsh says the best thing to do is to ignore the drumroll, the spotlight and the vertigo, and just stick to the basics.

"What you don't want," Walsh says, "is players thinking this will require something heroic. You don't want them thinking they have to do more. That's when the pressure can overwhelm them. Rather, they should be thinking: 'We've done this before. All we have to do is execute.' They should be calm and confident. If they are, every play becomes a high-percentage play.

"Of course," Walsh adds with a knowing smile, "it helps if you have Joe Montana at quarterback."

Indeed, it does. But as often as not, players who otherwise did not measure up to Montana's greatness have made memorable Super Bowl plays. "What you see in these games," says James Washington, a hero in the Dallas Cowboys' Super Bowl XXVIII victory, "is it isn't always the superstars who decide them. I was a role player, but years from now my grandchildren won't know that. They'll turn on the Super Bowl highlights and say, 'Look at Grandpa. He won the Super Bowl.' I'll sit there, drinking my lemonade and loving every minute of it."

On the following pages are accounts of 13 plays that had a profound impact on the Super Bowl.

SUPER BOWL
XXIII

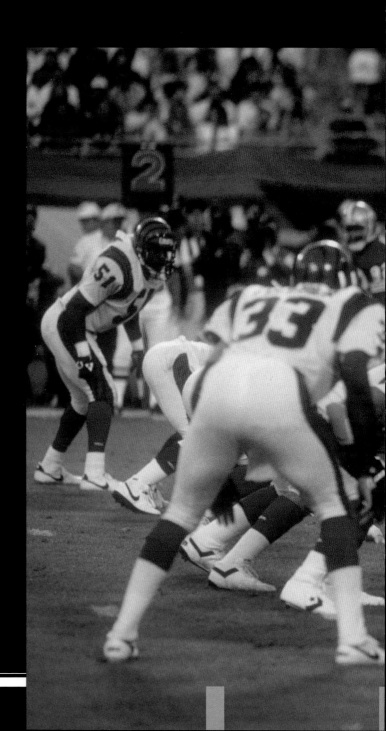

Joe Montana is the standard by which big play performers are measured. He threw 11 touchdown passes and no interceptions in leading the San Francisco 49ers to four wins in four Super Bowls. Bill Walsh was Montana's coach for the first three, including the 20-16 victory over Cincinnati in Super Bowl XXIII that culminated with Montana directing an 11-play, 92-yard drive to the winning touchdown, a 10-yard pass to John Taylor, with 34 seconds remaining.

That game, and that drive, were the final chapter of Walsh's pro coaching career, and the very essence of his quarterback, a man they called Joe Cool. It is now part of Super Bowl lore that as the 49ers were waiting to begin that final drive, trailing by three points with time running out, Montana calmly surveyed the scene at Miami's Joe Robbie Stadium and said: "Hey, check it out. There's John Candy."

Sure enough, John Candy was in the stands, eating popcorn, waiting along with the rest of the civilized world for the game to resume. "We looked over and it was like, 'John Candy, wow, that's cool,' " says 49ers tackle Harris Barton. "It broke the tension. Joe loosened things up. Then the ref blew his whistle, and Joe said 'OK, here we go.' The rest is history."

"I WAS IN FIVE SUPER BOWLS, AND THE GREATEST ONE WAS MY FIRST ONE, AGAINST CINCINNATI. THERE WERE ABOUT THREE MINUTES LEFT WHEN I CAME OFF THE FIELD, TOOK MY HELMET OFF, THREW MY GLOVES OFF. I WAS PHYSICALLY AND EMOTIONALLY DRAINED. ONLY THING I COULD DO WAS SIT THERE, THINKING WE WERE GONNA LOSE. JOE BEING JOE, HE TOLD EVERYBODY, 'COME ON. LET'S GO,' AND TOOK THEM OUT THERE. FIRST PLAY WE GOT A PENALTY. SECOND PLAY WE GOT ANOTHER PENALTY. I DIDN'T WATCH THE NEXT THREE PLAYS. THEN I STARTED HEARING THE CROWD, AND I'M GOING, 'WELL, MAYBE,' AND I LOOKED OUT THERE AGAIN. THE WORST FEELING WAS BEFORE WE STARTED MOVING THE BALL. THEN JERRY STARTED MAKING CATCHES, AND THAT CONFIDENCE LEVEL WENT BACK UP AGAIN. THEN WHEN J.T. CAUGHT THE BALL IN THE END ZONE, THAT WAS THE GREATEST FEELING. THAT'S ONE OF THE GREATEST SUPER BOWLS, BECAUSE IT WAS A STRUGGLE THE WHOLE GAME."

CHARLES HALEY, *defensive end, 49ers*

"I don't go up and down [emotionally]," Montana says. "I always felt relaxed was better. If you had too much emotion, it was harder to focus."

Montana's focus was so laser sharp—and his grasp of the Walsh offense so complete—that even though he began to hyperventilate during the final drive, he still led the team to a touchdown. Trying to call signals over the roar of the crowd made Montana so lightheaded, he almost blacked out. He threw the next pass away deliberately—his only incompletion on the drive—so he could have a moment to catch his breath. Like most things Montana tried on the field, it worked.

"There are a lot of people who play the game, but there aren't a lot of people who know how to play the game," says John Madden, who was the coach of the Oakland Raiders when they won Super Bowl XI. "Joe Montana knew how to play the game. Situations where other [quarterbacks] were frantic, Joe was cool. Where other guys were tight, Joe was loose. Where they were confused, he was in control. Part of it was the [Walsh] system, a perfect fit for him. And he had great players around him. But Joe was the guy who made it work. He seemed like a guy who'd been there before and knew how to handle it."

It is hard to quantify the degree to which a truly superior competitor, such as Montana, influences those high stakes moments. Certainly, he improves his team's chances,

and Walsh freely acknowledges he was the beneficiary of Montana's unique gifts. But Walsh also believes the system and how a team prepares over the course of a season has a lot to do with how it responds on Super Sunday. He questions the notion of "stepping up," as in, "the quarterback has to step up in this game." Better he should continue doing what he has done all year, Walsh says, and that applies to everyone on the team.

The setting may be extraordinary—the fireworks, the bombast, the celebrity glitter—but the task on the field should remain ordinary. There is bound to be anxiety—Barton talked about feeling like "a rabid dog" when he came on the field for the final drive against Cincinnati—but players can rise above that if they believe in what they are asked to do.

"That [winning] drive was the culmination of 10 years of planning and practice," Walsh said. "Every play was a play that we had practiced and rehearsed so many times. There were no miracles, no Hail Mary's, just a lot of 7- and 8-yard gains. There was only one pass longer than 20 yards (27 to Jerry Rice). We had run this [two-minute drill] countless times. Each man knew his responsibilities and carried them out."

> "THEY WERE BEATING US, WE WERE DOWN, AND JOE COMES INTO THE HUDDLE. I'M YELLING AND SCREAMING. 'COME ON, LET'S GO! IF WE WANT THE RING, WE'VE GOT TO GO OUT AND GET IT! THIS IS THE BIGGEST DRIVE OF MY LIFE!' JOE LOOKS AT ME—IT WAS DURING ONE OF THOSE LONG TV TIMEOUTS THEY HAVE IN THE SUPER BOWL—AND HE GOES, 'HEY H, CHECK IT OUT.' I GO, 'WHAT?' HE GOES, 'LOOK OVER THERE IN THAT END ZONE. THERE'S JOHN CANDY.' I LOOK, AND SURE ENOUGH JOHN CANDY IS SITTING THERE EATING SOME POPCORN.
>
> I LOOK BACK AT JOE, AND I LOOK AT THE CLOCK—THERE'S THREE MINUTES TO GO IN THE BIGGEST GAME OF THE YEAR—AND HE'S SO RELAXED. THEN ALL OF THE SUDDEN THE TV TIMEOUT ENDED, AND THE NEXT THING I KNOW WE'RE MARCHING DOWN THE FIELD FOR THE WINNING DRIVE.
>
> JOE PROBABLY DOESN'T EVEN REMEMBER SAYING IT, HE WAS SO RELAXED DURING THAT WHOLE SITUATION. YOU ALWAYS HEARD IT SAID THAT HE HAD ICE WATER RUNNING THROUGH HIS VEINS, AND I REALLY THINK HE DID. HE WAS THE MOST RELAXED AND POISED PERSON I'VE EVER MET."
>
> **HARRIS BARTON,** *offensive lineman, 49ers*

SUPER BOWL
XXXIV

Players do not have to be future Hall of Famers, like Joe Montana, or even Pro Bowl-quality performers to make a lasting mark on the Super Bowl. They can be journeymen like Mike Jones, the St. Louis Rams linebacker who was in his ninth NFL season, most of them spent as a special teams player, when he made the last-second tackle of Tennessee Titans wide receiver Kevin Dyson that preserved a 23-16 win in Super Bowl XXXIV.

Jones was playing the outside zone when Dyson and tight end Frank Wycheck ran a combination pattern from the Rams' 10-yard line. Jones shadowed Dyson, and when the Titans receiver caught a pass from Steve McNair, Jones dragged him down just short of the goal line. Wrote Ray Ratto in the *San Francisco Examiner*: "It was Jones, more than Kurt Warner and Isaac Bruce, who will be remembered in the five-second clips that define the

Super Bowl because he had the best five seconds of any player on the field."

"The smartest thing I did on that play was not over-try," Jones says. "If I had tried to put a kill shot on Dyson, he might have bounced off and gone in. I just wrapped him up and took him down, the old textbook tackle.

"It wasn't until after the game when Peter King [of *Sports Illustrated*] said, 'You're part of football history,' that I thought about it in those terms. The next week, I was on *Live With Regis and Kathie Lee*, I was on *The Charlie Rose Show*, I was the guy who made 'The Tackle.' The moral of the story is you have to make the most of your opportunities. You might have to wait a long time, like I did, and you might only get one shot, so you have to be prepared because you never know when it's going to be there."

"IF DYSON WOULD HAVE TAKEN IT UP TWO MORE YARDS VERTICALLY, HE WOULD HAVE CAUGHT THE BALL AND WALKED IN. IT WAS A 5-YARD SLANT. DICE CUT IT SHORT BY ABOUT TWO YARDS."

STEVE McNAIR, *quarterback, Titans*

"WHEN HE FIRST HIT ME, I THOUGHT I COULD RUN THROUGH HIS ARM. I'M THINKING, 'IF I CAN GET THROUGH THIS ...' THEN ALL OF A SUDDEN MY FEET STOPPED. ALL I NEEDED WAS ONE MORE STEP, BUT I COULDN'T GET MY LEFT LEG MOVING. EVEN WHEN I WAS GOING DOWN, IT SEEMED LIKE THAT END ZONE WAS SO CLOSE. AFTER THE GAME, SOMEBODY SAID IT WAS A PERFECT TACKLE."

KEVIN DYSON, *wide receiver, Titans*

SUPER BOWL
I

"THAT INTERCEPTION WAS THE KEY PLAY OF THE GAME. IT CHANGED THE PERSONALITY OF THE GAME. BEFORE THAT PLAY, AND TOUCHDOWN, WE WERE DOING THE THINGS WE WANTED TO DO. YOU DON'T LIKE TO THINK THAT ONE PLAY CAN MAKE THAT MUCH DIFFERENCE, BUT IT SEEMED TO. FROM THAT POINT, WE HAD TO PLAY CATCH-UP. WE HAD TO PASS MORE AND DO THINGS WE DON'T NORMALLY DO BEST." **HANK STRAM,** *coach, Chiefs*

Sometimes the big plays were obvious, as in the case of the Joe Montana-led touchdown drive in Super Bowl XXIII and the Mike Jones tackle in Super Bowl XXXIV. But there were other games that ended in lopsided scores, yet turned on one critical play. The man who made the play may not have left with the MVP award or made the trip to Disney World, but he, too, delivered in the clutch.

In the first Super Bowl, the Green Bay Packers overwhelmed the Kansas City Chiefs, 35-10. On paper, it looks like a blowout, and what most remember about the game is rogue receiver Max McGee partying all night and then catching two touchdown passes from MVP Bart Starr. The truth is, the Packers, lords of the mighty NFL, were in a sweat at halftime as they went to the locker room with a tenuous 14-10 lead. The Chiefs, upstarts from the AFL, were a much tougher challenge than anyone expected.

"All of a sudden, this team that most people thought was a joke wasn't a joke anymore," says Bill Curry, the Green Bay center. "They played us almost even for 30 minutes, and they were gaining confidence. I remember the look on Coach Lombardi's face. He was worried. We all were worried."

Vince Lombardi was worried enough that he put his defense in a blitzing scheme for the second half. Lombardi normally was scornful of the blitz—"The weapon of weaklings," he called it. He believed in pressuring the quarterback the old-fashioned way, with four linemen. But after watching quarterback Len Dawson operate effectively in Kansas City's floating pocket, Lombardi swallowed his pride and instructed linebackers Dave Robinson and Lee Roy Caffey to blitz on the first third-down situation of the second half.

"They caught us in a blocking scheme where we were unprotected from my left side," Dawson says. "They surprised us. All of a sudden, I had this pressure in my face and I made a critical mistake. I tried to get the ball to [tight end] Fred Arbanas. I never saw Willie Wood."

Wood, Green Bay's free safety, played it perfectly. Floating in the middle of the field, he read the pattern and broke to the ball the instant it left Dawson's hand. Wood cut in front of Arbanas, made the interception and returned the ball 50 yards to the Kansas City 5-yard line. On the next play, halfback Elijah Pitts scored. Green Bay was ahead, 21-10, and the Chiefs were never in the game again.

"I should've held the ball or thrown it up into the stands," Dawson says. "That was the turning point. At halftime,

we really felt like we were going to win the game, but the interception deflated us. Give the Packers credit. Vince made the call, and Willie made the play. That's why they were a great team."

Wood says, "The funny thing about it is, for such a big play, it was so easy. It was like Lenny threw the ball right to me. I wasn't looking to make a big play. I wasn't the kind of safety who took a lot of chances—Vince didn't allow it. He believed in each man carrying out his assignment. If you do that, you'll get your opportunities to make the big plays. But if you try to force it, that's when you make a big mistake."

"THE FEELING I HAD WHEN WE WENT INTO THE DRESSING ROOM AT HALFTIME WAS THAT THEY HADN'T DOMINATED US AND WE HAD MOVED THE BALL. I WAS VERY EAGER TO PLAY THE SECOND HALF. NOW THE BIG ISSUE WAS: WHAT ADJUSTMENTS WOULD GREEN BAY MAKE IN THE SECOND HALF, AND WHAT ADJUSTMENTS WOULD WE MAKE?

WHEN LEN THREW THE INTERCEPTION, IT JUST STARTED TUMBLING AWAY FROM US. IT WAS TOUGH TO CATCH UP BECAUSE THEY WERE A VERY SOUND TEAM AND DIDN'T GIVE UP MANY POINTS. AS GOOD AS THEIR OFFENSE WAS, I THINK THEIR DEFENSE WAS EVEN BETTER. ABOUT MIDWAY THROUGH THE THIRD QUARTER, I SAID, 'CHANCES ARE NOT GREAT WE'RE GONNA WIN THIS GAME. BUT, BY GOD, THEY'RE NOT MUCH BETTER THAN US.'"

MIKE GARRETT, *running back, Chiefs*

SUPER BOWL
XXI

The story of Super Bowl XXI would seem to begin and end with New York Giants quarterback Phil Simms. He had one of the greatest passing days in Super Bowl history, completing 22 of 25 attempts for 268 yards and three touchdowns in the 39-20 victory over the Denver Broncos. However, Broncos quarterback John Elway insists that the game turned in the second quarter on a goal-line stand by the Giants defense.

Denver was leading, 10-7, and Elway was driving the Broncos toward a touchdown. They were at the Giants'

Elway felt the game was decided on that goal line series.

"If we had scored there," Elway says, "it would have been a different game."

It was not a Herculean effort by one player taking it upon himself to save the day, nor was it a victory fueled by raw emotion. There was no pep talk, no adjustment in strategy. It was just a great team—in this case, the Giants defense— doing what it had done all season: Imposing its will and muscle on the opposition. The Giants had the league's No. 1 defense that season, and they shut out the Washington

1-yard line and had four chances to score. On first down, Elway tried to sweep around right end and was tackled by Lawrence Taylor for a 1-yard loss. On second down, Gerald Willhite ran up the middle and was stopped cold by Harry Carson. On third down, coach Dan Reeves called for a sweep by halfback Sammy Winder, and Carl Banks dropped him for a 4-yard loss.

If those failed running attempts were not demoralizing enough, kicker Rich Karlis was wide right on a 23-yard field goal attempt, the shortest miss in Super Bowl history. Instead of extending their lead, the Broncos opened the door to a Giants' comeback. New York scored the next 26 points as Simms passed his way into the record book. But

Redskins, 17-0, in the NFC Championship Game. Washington had 18 opportunities on third or fourth down, and none resulted in a first down.

"All year we were beating people up and breaking them down," says Banks, a superb outside linebacker who often was overshadowed by Taylor, his Hall of Fame teammate. "Denver ran a lot of screen passes and quarterback draws, stuff that had us off-balance. But once they got down to the goal line, we drew a line in the sand. We said, 'These SOBs are not going to score.'

"At that point, we put our stamp on the game. We took them on, man to man, and brought the hammer down. Three straight plays, we stuffed them. When that series

ended, we looked them in the eye and said, 'We own you.' From that point on, it was no contest."

The Giants defense stayed with the normal scheme drawn up by coach Bill Parcells and defensive coordinator Bill Belichick. They studied tape of their regular season victory over Denver, a hard-fought 19-16 decision at Giants Stadium. Banks noted the one Broncos' touchdown came on a Winder sweep, so when it was third and goal in the Super Bowl, Banks kept his eye on Winder.

"Their line didn't block as hard on plays going away," Banks says, "so I was able to get inside the tight end and get the angle on Winder. That's the thing about big plays. They don't just happen, and you don't just get lucky. On that series, our execution was perfect."

Banks agrees there is such a thing as "big-play psychology." Some players, he says, thrive in pressure situations. Others hesitate and, therefore, fail. Sports psychologists have a term for it: fear paralysis. It can be as debilitating as a torn hamstring.

"I never felt it, I know L.T. didn't feel it," Banks says. "So much of this game, or any game, is mental. Why do you think Michael Jordan wanted the ball at the end of every game? Because he really believed he'd make the shot. That's where it all starts, with that belief."

"EARLIER IN THE YEAR AGAINST US THEY HAD SCORED ON A PITCHOUT FROM FOUR YARDS OUT. I EXPECTED THAT PLAY AGAIN, AND THAT'S WHAT THEY CALLED. THEY HAD A SLASHING TYPE OF RUNNING GAME. YOU HAD A SPLIT SECOND TO MAKE YOUR READ, AND THAT'S IT; GIVE THEM TWO YARDS AND THEY WERE GONE. I DIDN'T HAVE TIME TO SQUARE UP ON WINDER AND MAKE A FORM TACKLE. I JUST GOT MY HEAD IN THERE AND MADE THE HIT. I HAD ZIGZAGS IN MY EYES FOR THE REST OF THE HALF.

THEY DIDN'T GET AWAY FROM THEIR TENDENCIES. I HAD STUDIED A LOT OF FILM. I REMEMBER HEARING HOWIE LONG ON HBO, AND HE SAID, 'A WORD OF ADVICE: STUDY FILM AS MUCH AS YOU CAN.' SO I STUDIED."

CARL BANKS, *linebacker, Giants*

SUPER BOWL
XVII

"WE KNEW IF WE DIDN'T MAKE IT THEN, IT WOULD BE A RISKY FIELD GOAL. WE DECIDED TO TAKE OUR BEST PLAY AND GO AT THEM. WE DIDN'T WANT TO LOSE A SUPER BOWL BY NOT BEING TOUGH ENOUGH. THE PLAY WAS A FAKE ZOOM. I THINK THEY THOUGHT WE WERE SLANTING ONE WAY AND GOT CAUGHT WHEN WE WENT THE OTHER WAY."

JOE GIBBS, *coach, Redskins*

S ome players relish the spotlight more than others. The bigger the game, the larger the audience, the better they are apt to perform. Joe Bugel, the Washington Redskins offensive line coach in the 1980s, calls it "football arrogance," and he points to John Riggins, the Hall of Fame running back, as someone who wore it like a suit of armor.

"We'd come out for warm-ups, and John would be checking the house," Bugel says. "He'd say, 'How many people are here today?' I'd say, 'Sixty thousand, seventy thousand, something like that.' He'd say, 'They're all here to see me, so tell Joe [Gibbs, the head coach] to give me the ball.' John wanted it all on his shoulders, and the bigger the game, the more he wanted it."

There was no bigger game in Redskins' history than Super Bowl XVII. Washington played the Miami Dolphins in front of 103,667 fans at the Rose Bowl. Riggins had rushed for 444 yards in three playoff victories preceding the Super Bowl. It was the first Super Bowl for the Redskins under Gibbs. They were up against a team that was coached by Don Shula and held a significant edge in experience and pedigree.

Entering the fourth quarter, Miami led, 17-13. With 10 minutes remaining, Washington had fourth-and-1 at the Dolphins' 43-yard line. Gibbs never hesitated. He called for "70 Chip," the team's best short-yardage play. It was a two tight-end formation, with Riggins, a 6-foot-2, 250-pound battering ram, following lead blocker Otis Wonsley off the left side.

"Everyone in North America knew what was coming," Riggins says. "I might as well have held up a sign that read, 'I'm getting the ball.' But it's one thing to know something's coming, and it's another thing to stop it. We only needed a yard, and I knew the Hogs [Washington's offensive line] could get me that. As it turned out, we got a whole lot more."

Bugel says, "We had great confidence in the play. We ran it against 12 and 13 [defenders] in practice and still made

yardage. It was our bread-and-butter. On this play, [tackle Joe] Jacoby and [guard Russ] Grimm got great blocks, and John cut right off [tight end] Donnie Warren's butt.

"We used to tell John, 'We can block 10 guys, but there's always gonna be one guy we can't block because of the quarterback. That's your guy, you have to beat him.' In this case, it was the cornerback [Don] McNeal."

Center Jeff Bostic says, "Whenever John broke through to the second level clean, like he did on that play, he was

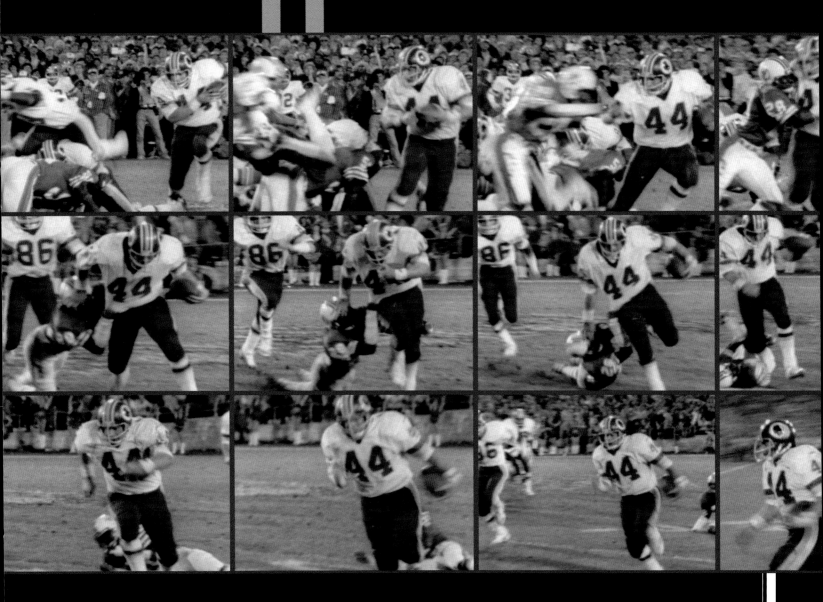

unstoppable. He would punish those defensive backs. I can't imagine what goes through the mind of a 190-pound safety that has to take on that big diesel. He would run through those guys and never break stride."

The 5-foot-11, 180-pound McNeal got a piece of Riggins' jersey, but he did not even slow him down. Riggins broke free on a 43-yard touchdown run that gave the Redskins their first lead. They scored again on their next possession—Riggins carried the ball on eight of 12 plays—

to make the final score 27-17. Riggins finished with 166 yards on 38 rushing attempts, both Super Bowl records at the time. (Two players since have rushed for more yards, but Riggins still holds the attempts record.)

"When I see the film of that run," Bugel says, "and I see the close-up of John's face, God, it's awesome. The look on his face, the intensity, that's what won the game. '70 Chip'—that play is etched in stone."

PITTSBURGH 31, LOS ANGELES RAMS 19

SUPER BOWL XIV

The Pittsburgh Steelers won their fourth Super Bowl by successfully executing a play that virtually no one on the team believed would work. Coach Chuck Noll knew better, and he insisted on calling the play. A Hall of Fame quarterback (Terry Bradshaw) and a Hall of Fame wide receiver (John Stallworth) made it work.

The Steelers were losing, 19-17, to the underdog Los Angeles Rams early in the fourth quarter of Super Bowl XIV when Noll called for "60-Prevent-Slot-Hook-And-Go," a long pass pattern. The team had run the play regularly in practice the previous week and never connected. Bradshaw had so little confidence in the play that he had refused to run it the first time Noll called for it in the Super Bowl.

With 12 minutes remaining, and the Rams defense—coached by former Steelers assistant Bud Carson—choking off the middle zones, Noll again ordered Bradshaw to throw deep. Lynn Swann, the hero of Super Bowl X, had suffered a concussion and was out of the game, leaving Stallworth as Pittsburgh's only deep threat, which meant that he was sure to draw double coverage. Bradshaw, who had thrown three interceptions, was willing to trust his coach's judgment this time.

"I should've been bombing away earlier," Bradshaw says. "We could've beaten them by going deep. That was our strength and their weakness. Their secondary wasn't that good. We played into their hands by throwing underneath. But they were set up for the long ball. Stall faked the hook, the safety [Eddie Brown] bit on it, and Stall was one-on-one with the corner [Rod Perry]. I just let it fly."

Bradshaw's pass was perfect. It cleared Perry's

outstretched hand, and Stallworth caught the ball over his shoulder and raced away to complete a 73-yard touchdown that put the Steelers ahead, 24-19.

Steelers linebacker Jack Lambert intercepted a Vince Ferragamo pass that set up a Franco Harris touchdown in the closing minutes and made the final score a deceptive 31-19. It was a much closer game than that, and the decisive play was the Bradshaw to Stallworth bomb.

That was characteristic of Bradshaw, who was in many ways the anti-Joe Montana, yet shared the same bottom line: four Super Bowl appearances, four victories. Bradshaw

was high-strung; Montana was calm. Bradshaw made mistakes and turned the ball over; Montana did not. But in the fourth quarter, when the game was on the line, both quarterbacks were at their best. Bradshaw threw a touchdown pass in the fourth quarter of each of his Super Bowls. In those fourth quarters, he averaged a stunning 26.5 yards per completion and did not throw an interception.

"I could play in the big games. I was supremely confident in big games," Bradshaw says. "Go to each of our Super Bowls: that pass to Stallworth, the [touchdown] passes to Swann, the [touchdown] pass to Larry Brown—that's who I

"WHEN I CAME IN, THE OFFENSE WAS VERY MUCH IN THE MINORITY ON THE STEELERS. WE PLAYED GOOD, STRONG DEFENSE, AND WE RAN THE FOOTBALL, CONTROLLED THE FOOTBALL. WITH TERRY BRADSHAW'S EMERGENCE AS A QUARTERBACK, AND SWANN AND I BECOMING MORE MATURE AS RECEIVERS, WE DEVELOPED MORE WEAPONS THAT WE COULD USE, AND CHUCK

am. In the fourth quarter of those games, I came through.

"Forget all the other junk, the [regular season] games that don't make a difference. It's all about winning championships, and the other players knew they could depend on me. They knew what I was about. Most accurate passer in the NFL? Not even close. But it's not about statistics. Winning championships is the measure of every player in any sport. We did that, and we did it together. That's what I treasure. That's what I take to my grave."

Bradshaw's ability was considerable, but the collective ability of his Pittsburgh teammates was part of the equation, as well. He was taking the snap from a Hall of Fame center (Mike Webster), handing off to a Hall of Fame running back (Franco Harris) and throwing to two Hall of Fame receivers (Swann and Stallworth).

"It gives you a tremendous feeling of confidence, knowing those guys are there for you," Bradshaw says. "Did you ever sit on a great horse and feel that power? That's about what it's like. And I was lucky enough to ride that horse in four Super Bowls. It doesn't get any better than that."

NOLL SAW THE WISDOM IN USING THEM. WE WERE MUCH MORE OFFENSIVE-MINDED IN THOSE LAST TWO SUPER BOWLS. THE BIG PLAY WAS ALWAYS A POSSIBILITY. IN FACT, WE WON THE LAST ONE ON THE BIG PLAY. THE GROUND GAME WAS GONE, AND WE HAD TO RELY ON GETTING UP TOP AND COMING UP WITH SOME BIG ONES."

JOHN STALLWORTH, *wide receiver, Steelers*

BALTIMORE 16, DALLAS 13

SUPER BOWL V

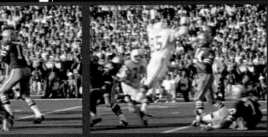

T he Dallas Cowboys and the Baltimore Colts combined for 11 turnovers, including a record six interceptions, in Super Bowl V. The most important interception was made by Colts safety Rick Volk midway through the fourth quarter.

Baltimore was trailing, 13-6, and Earl Morrall had replaced injured Johnny Unitas (torn rib cartilage) at quarterback. The Colts offense was unable to move against

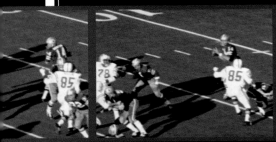

the Cowboys' Doomsday Defense. They were running out of time—and hope—when Volk intercepted a Craig Morton pass and returned it 30 yards to the Dallas 3-yard line. Two plays later, fullback Tom Nowatzke scored a touchdown, and Jim O'Brien kicked the extra point to tie the score.

In the final minute, an interception by linebacker Mike Curtis set up O'Brien's 32-yard field goal that gave the Colts a 16-13 victory.

Volk's interception got the Colts back in the game. "We were frustrated all day," Morrall says. "That play let us punch in a touchdown. It really lifted us."

Volk says, "Roy Hinton did most of the work. He got a good rush, and he had his hands up, so Morton had to throw the ball higher than he wanted. It bounced off [fullback] Walt Garrison's fingers and fell right to me. All I had to do was run with it."

PITTSBURGH 21, DALLAS 17

SUPER BOWL

> "THEY RUSHED 10 MEN AND SOMEBODY MISSED A BLOCK. I DON'T KNOW WHO IT WAS. WE PROBABLY JUST BRUSH-BLOCKED HARRISON, AND HE MADE THE BIG PLAY. THAT'S WHAT USUALLY HAPPENS ON A BLOCKED PUNT."
>
> **TOM LANDRY,** *coach, Cowboys*

With 11 minutes remaining, the Pittsburgh Steelers trailed the Dallas Cowboys, 10-7, in Super Bowl X. Steelers coach Chuck Noll departed from his usual strategy and called for an all-out 10-man rush at punter Mitch Hoopes, hoping for a blocked kick.

Reserve fullback Reggie Harrison had never blocked a kick, not even in high school, but he blocked this one. The ball struck Harrison in the face and split his tongue, but he said it was worth the pain to see the ball roll out of the end zone for a safety that cut the Dallas lead to 10-9.

More than that, wrote Phil Musick in the *Pittsburgh Post-Gazette*, the play "seemed to strip the Cowboys of their confidence."

"I could see the balloon collapsing right then," said Dallas defensive tackle Jethro Pugh.

During the next eight minutes, the Steelers scored 12 points (two field goals and a touchdown) and took the lead for the first time. They won, 21-17, for their second consecutive Super Bowl triumph.

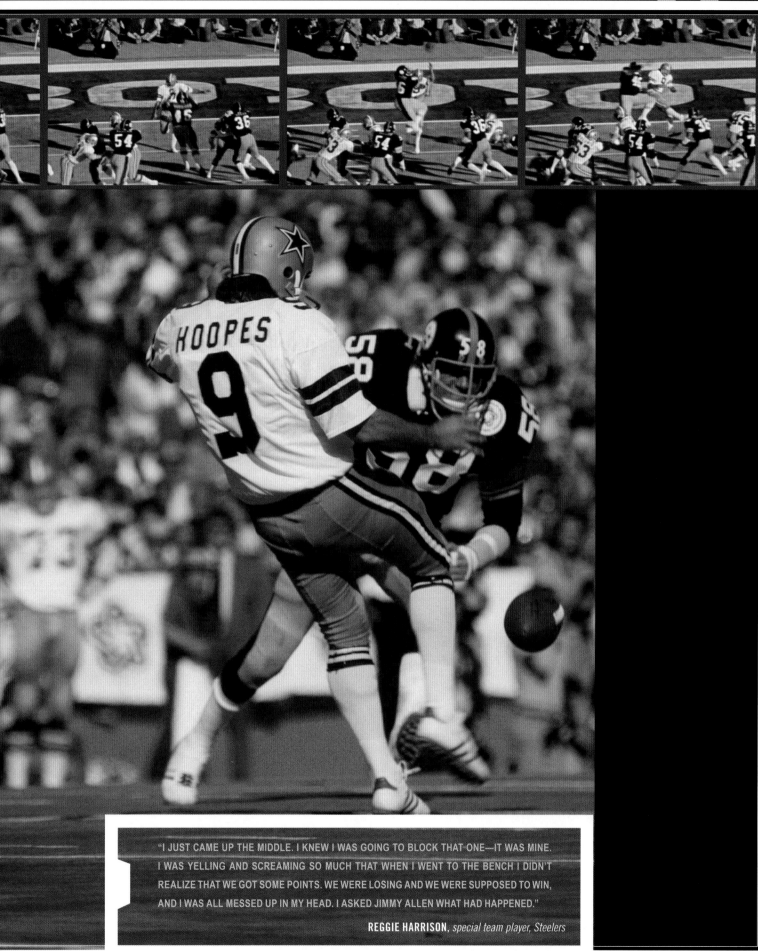

"I JUST CAME UP THE MIDDLE. I KNEW I WAS GOING TO BLOCK THAT ONE—IT WAS MINE.
I WAS YELLING AND SCREAMING SO MUCH THAT WHEN I WENT TO THE BENCH I DIDN'T
REALIZE THAT WE GOT SOME POINTS. WE WERE LOSING AND WE WERE SUPPOSED TO WIN,
AND I WAS ALL MESSED UP IN MY HEAD. I ASKED JIMMY ALLEN WHAT HAD HAPPENED."

REGGIE HARRISON, *special team player, Steelers*

OAKLAND 27, PHILADELPHIA 10

SUPER BOWL
XV

A huge momentum swing late in the first quarter of Super Bowl XV helped the Oakland Raiders defeat the Philadelphia Eagles, 27-10, in the Louisiana Superdome. Trailing 7-0, the Eagles appeared to tie the score on a 40-yard pass from Ron Jaworski to wide receiver Rodney Parker. However, the play was nullified by an illegal motion penalty called against the other receiver, Harold Carmichael.

The Eagles were forced to punt, and the Raiders gained possession at their 14-yard line. Three plays later, Jim Plunkett lofted a pass over the frantic reach of cornerback Herman Edwards and into the arms of fullback Kenny King, who raced 80 yards to a touchdown. Instead of a 7-7 deadlock, the Eagles found themselves in a 14-point hole that they never escaped.

"If we would have made a couple of big plays early, we would have been OK," said Eagles coach Dick Vermeil. "But we fell behind, and we seemed to sag emotionally.

"The play to King really hurt. If you look at the film, you see [defensive end] Carl Hairston is one step away from sacking Plunkett and he is pulled down by the face mask. It's an obvious holding penalty. The official is right there, but there's no call."

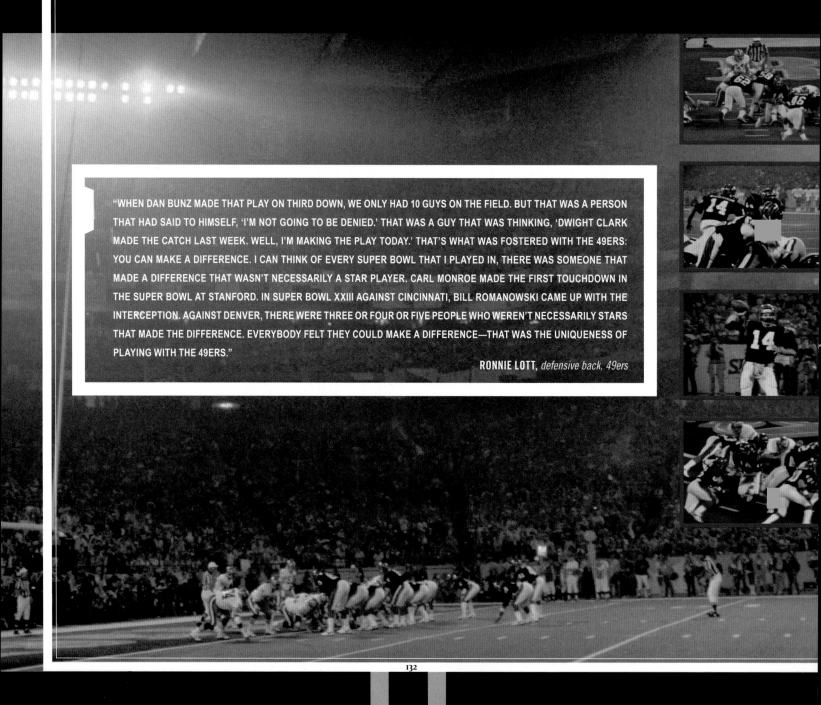

SUPER BOWL
XVI

J oe Montana won the first of his three Super Bowl MVP awards in Super Bowl XVI, but the outcome was really decided by the San Francisco 49ers defense, which stopped the Cincinnati Bengals at the goal line on four consecutive plays late in the third quarter.

The 49ers were leading, 20-7, but the Bengals had scored a touchdown on their previous possession, and their defense had stymied Montana the entire period. When the

"WHEN DAN BUNZ MADE THAT PLAY ON THIRD DOWN, WE ONLY HAD 10 GUYS ON THE FIELD. BUT THAT WAS A PERSON THAT HAD SAID TO HIMSELF, 'I'M NOT GOING TO BE DENIED.' THAT WAS A GUY THAT WAS THINKING, 'DWIGHT CLARK MADE THE CATCH LAST WEEK. WELL, I'M MAKING THE PLAY TODAY.' THAT'S WHAT WAS FOSTERED WITH THE 49ERS: YOU CAN MAKE A DIFFERENCE. I CAN THINK OF EVERY SUPER BOWL THAT I PLAYED IN, THERE WAS SOMEONE THAT MADE A DIFFERENCE THAT WASN'T NECESSARILY A STAR PLAYER. CARL MONROE MADE THE FIRST TOUCHDOWN IN THE SUPER BOWL AT STANFORD. IN SUPER BOWL XXIII AGAINST CINCINNATI, BILL ROMANOWSKI CAME UP WITH THE INTERCEPTION. AGAINST DENVER, THERE WERE THREE OR FOUR OR FIVE PEOPLE WHO WEREN'T NECESSARILY STARS THAT MADE THE DIFFERENCE. EVERYBODY FELT THEY COULD MAKE A DIFFERENCE—THAT WAS THE UNIQUENESS OF PLAYING WITH THE 49ERS."

RONNIE LOTT, *defensive back, 49ers*

Bengals drove to the San Francisco 3-yard line, the team's confidence had gained the momentum of an avalanche.

But the 49ers kept the Bengals out of the end zone. Pete Johnson, a punishing 260-pound fullback, failed to budge the defense on first, second and fourth downs. The third-down play was a swing pass from quarterback Ken Anderson to halfback Charles Alexander. Linebacker Dan Bunz slammed Alexander to the turf just short of the goal line.

"Twenty times out of twenty, that play is a touchdown," said Chuck Studley, the 49ers defensive coordinator. "But Bunz read it perfectly and made a great hit. He put his hat right through [Alexander's] spinal column."

Bunz and fellow linebacker Jack Reynolds combined to stop Johnson on fourth down, and the 49ers held on to win their first NFL championship, 26-21.

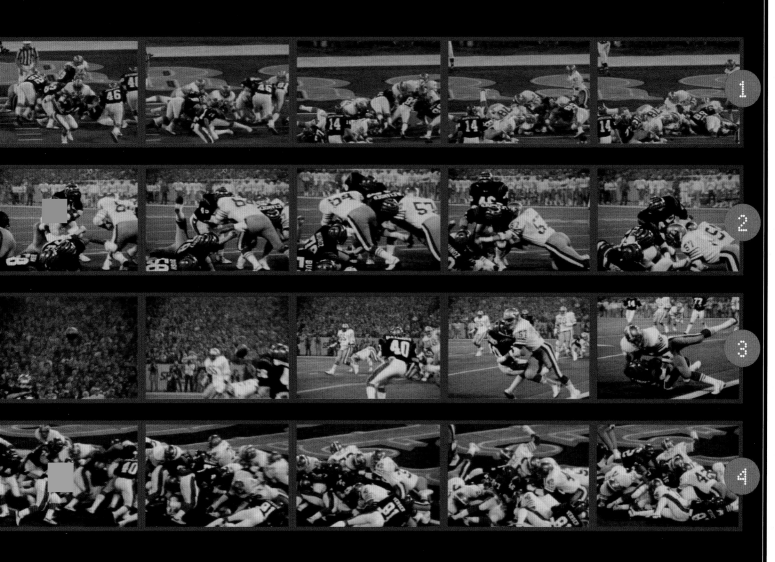

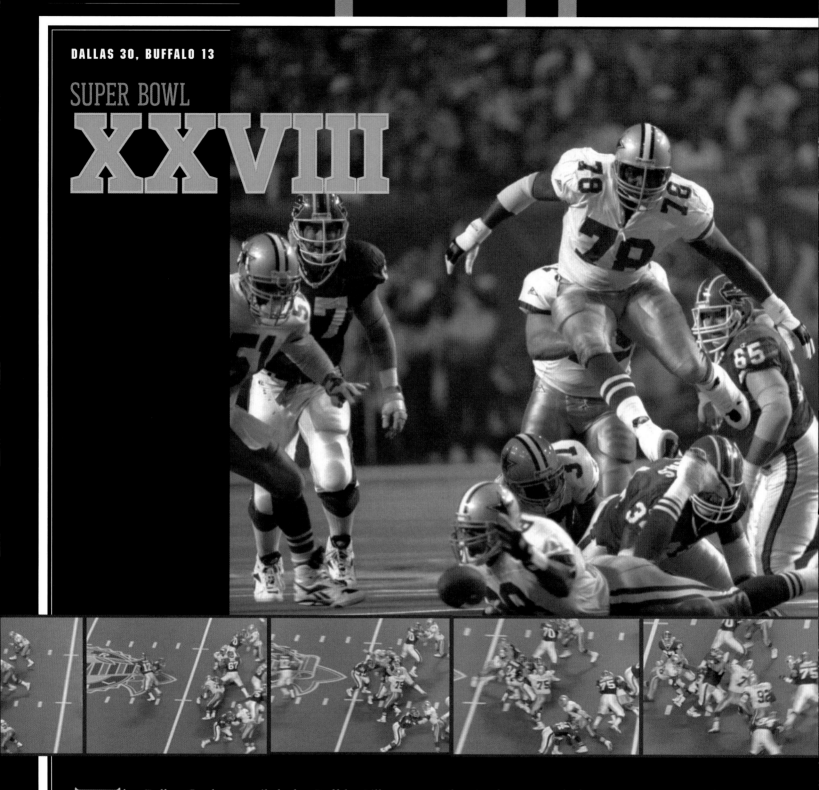

DALLAS 30, BUFFALO 13

SUPER BOWL

XXVIII

The Dallas Cowboys trailed the Buffalo Bills, 13-6, at the start of the second half of Super Bowl XXVIII. Dallas safety James Washington soon made a play that changed the tone of the game. He pounced on a fumble by Thurman Thomas and returned the ball 46-yards for a touchdown that tied the score.

The Cowboys scored the next 17 points and won decisively, 30-13. "I had a feeling it was my day," Washington said. "I told Michael Irvin and Ken Norton before the game, 'This is my day.' I had studied the Buffalo offense. I knew their formations and patterns cold. I said, 'I know everything they're going to run.' I woke up that morning at

six, and my mind was racing. I couldn't wait to play."

Washington made three big plays in the game. He forced a fumble by Thomas in the first quarter that set up a Dallas field goal, and he intercepted a pass that led to the Cowboys' final touchdown. He also made 11 tackles. But it was Washington's fumble recovery in the third quarter that made the difference.

"Daryl Johnston hugged me after I scored," Washington said, referring to the Dallas fullback. "He said, 'That was what we needed.' I think that play did two things: It gave our team a spark, and at the same time it started the Bills thinking, 'Oh no, not again.'"

SUPER BOWL

Desmond Howard became the first special teams player to earn the MVP award in a Super Bowl. His 99-yard touchdown on a fourth-quarter kickoff return helped the Green Bay Packers defeat the New England Patriots, 35-21.

The Packers led most of the game, but the young Patriots, under the direction of coach Bill Parcells, kept coming back. They closed the gap to 27-21 on a touchdown run by Curtis Martin, and seemed to have wrested the momentum from Green Bay.

But on the ensuing kickoff, Howard, the former Heisman Trophy winner from the University of Michigan, broke loose and dashed the Patriots' hopes. It was the longest kickoff return in Super Bowl history. Howard also had punt returns of 32 and 34 yards. He finished with 244 yards in return yardage.

SUPER BOWL

Everyone remembers how Super Bowl XXXVI ended: Adam Vinatieri kicked a 48-yard field goal to provide the New England Patriots with a 20-17 victory over the St. Louis Rams. And some remember Tom Brady's 23-yard completion to Troy Brown that got the Patriots across midfield.

But the biggest play in New England's drive that led to Vinatieri's field goal—and the Patriots' first Super Bowl championship—was the fourth play. On second-and-10 from the New England 30, Brady threw a safety valve pass to halfback J.R. Redmond. He picked up 11 yards and a first down, and, equally important, got out of bounds to stop the clock with 33 seconds remaining.

Until that play, Patriots offensive coordinator Charlie

Weis was uncertain about trying to win the game in regulation time. When the Patriots got the ball at their 17 with 1:21 left, John Madden said in the ABC broadcast booth that they should play for overtime. "You don't want to take any chances," Madden said.

Weis knew better than to take chances, but he was not willing to sit on the ball, either. He had Brady throw a few safe passes, hoping they would gain enough ground to put the team in field goal range. Redmond's play enabled the Patriots to press onward.

"To be honest with you," Weis said, "if he had gotten tackled in bounds right away, we probably would have kneeled on it and gone into overtime, because then you're still on your own 30 and you're trying to rush things."

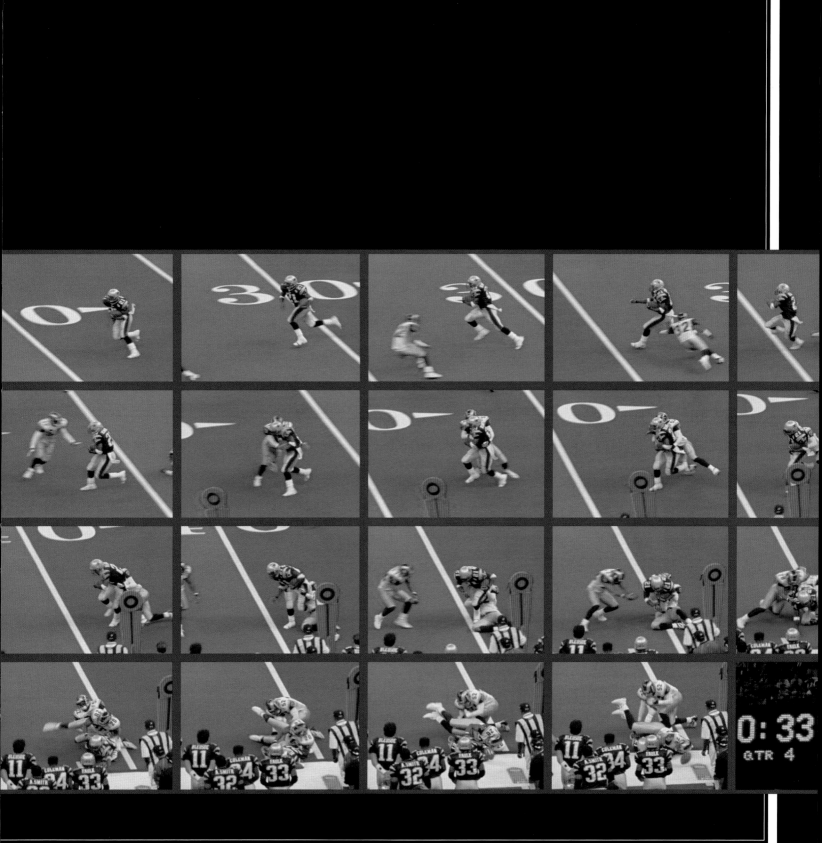

BRADY

The Super Bowl is a huge event. The stakes don't get any higher. But when you run out onto the field for a two-minute drill in that game—or any game, really—you don't think about the stakes.

When I took the field with 1:30 remaining in Super Bowl XXXVI—the biggest game I had ever played in; it was my second NFL season—I was just focused on what had to be accomplished. You realize the situation. The score: We were in a 17–17 tie with the St. Louis Rams. The time: We didn't have any timeouts left.

You're not thinking about the pressure. At least I'm not thinking about the pressure. I'm not thinking about, "What happens if I throw an interception?" Or "What happens if we stall on downs?" It's "What happens if they blitz me?" Or "What happens if they play this coverage?" In a lot of ways, it was very much something that I had experienced before. I had worked on two-minute drills in practice. We had been halfway decent at this during the 2001 season.

I looked at it as a great opportunity. Would you rather be kneeling on the ball at the end of a 49–3 blowout? A lot of people might say, "Yeah, sure." But it's a great opportunity when it's a two-minute drill because that's the true test of a team, and the true test of the leadership on a team. Can you get the guys down the field in a short amount of time, with the stakes at their highest?—that's really what playing quarterback is all about.

Against the Rams, we were up 17–3 at one point, and then everything happened so fast to get to 17–17.

We could have taken the safe way out and sat on the ball, and taken our chances in overtime. A lot of people felt that might have been the best strategy. John Madden

thought so, and shared that opinion with millions and millions of television viewers. But in that situation, I don't think you want the Rams to get the ball. They're a very explosive team, and they had scored on the previous two possessions in a short amount of time.

I walked over to Charlie Weis, our offensive coordinator, and said, "Are we going?" He said he would check with our head coach, Bill Belichick. I went to warm up, and Charlie came back and said, "Yeah, we're going."

That was a great opportunity for us to have the ball at the end of the game. Before the game, if you would have told our team it would have been a tie ballgame with 1:30 left (1:21 when I took the first snap from the shotgun formation) and we would have the ball with a chance to win it, I'm sure everyone would have jumped at that. What more could you ask for?

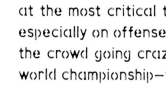

I completed six passes to move us from our own 17-yard line to the St. Louis 30. Then, with seven seconds left, Adam Vinatieri kicked a 48-yard field goal to give us the win.

Two years later, in Super Bowl XXXVIII, we faced the same situation against the Carolina Panthers. The score was tied, 29–29. We took the field at our 40, after John Kasay had kicked off out of bounds, with 1:08 remaining. This time we had all three of our timeouts, and we used them while driving to the Panthers' 23. With nine seconds left, Adam came through again, kicking the winning field goal from 41 yards.

You can draw on your experience from two years before, but I also was drawing on the practice I had the Friday before the Carolina game. We practice those two-minute drills every week, and you gain confidence every week in practice that you can go out there and run those plays and go down the field and score in a quick enough time. I had the confidence to say, "I've been in this situation, and I know what I can do here and I know we've done this before." But at the same time, it's still very unpredictable. There are a lot of things that could happen every single play. To think you can go out there and succeed just because you've done it before, I don't really believe that's true.

It's impossible for one guy to do it alone. You need the entire group to do their best at the most critical time. Everybody has to be on the same page on every single play, especially on offense. When you can accomplish that, and it's so hectic around you—with the crowd going crazy, and a defense that's really intense, and you're playing for the world championship—we're all very proud of that.

You can look in a person's eyes in the huddle and know if they're intimidated, or if they don't have confidence. You'd better have confidence out there as a player because if you don't have it in yourself, you can't expect anyone else to have it in you.

That was the sort of confidence that you saw from Joe Montana in the Super Bowl, and in every game he played, for that matter. When you grow up in the Bay Area during those times, as I did, every kid wanted to be Joe Montana. There was such a presence that he had, and it was reflected in the way he talked, the way he walked. Everything in his mannerisms made it seem as if he was in control. And he was. That was why he always performed so well. He had a tremendous amount of confidence in himself, as he should have, because he was one of the best quarterbacks of all time.

Now I will admit, there's always a little bit of nerves. There's always a little part of your stomach that's uneasy because you're competing at that level and you can't take anything for granted. As much as you'd like to think you can project the outcome of the game, you can't. You can really only have the confidence to believe that, "Man, we can go out and win this game." Or, "I can go out and play at a championship level."

At the same time, you haven't done it, and I think that uneasiness is from a little bit of unpredictability. That doesn't really reflect on the confidence that you have. You have the confidence to go out there, and when you do look in those guys' eyes, they look back at you and realize, "Man, I like the guy that's leading us. And if we're all able to do our job, he'll come through, as well." You have a certain way as a player, and if all of a sudden, with 1:30 left, you change the way you look or the way you're talking, if your voice is cracking, I'm sure all those guys will be thinking: "Oh, no, we're in deep trouble here." It should be business as usual.

Every time I step into the huddle with those guys, I'm trying to prove myself to them. I look at those guys probably the same way they look at me. I'm expecting them to go out and do their job. I'm not asking Matt Light to throw a pass; I'm just asking him to block his guy. He's not asking me to block anybody; he just wants me to throw the ball to the guy that's most open. The receiver has to get open and catch the ball. The running back has to stay in pass protection and block, and if he gets out, he has to be able to do something with the ball. There's a lot of trust, and the only way it works is if there's trust in everybody out there on the field.

When you get to the Super Bowl, you have to be doing something right. You're not going to go out there and change what you've been doing over the course of an entire season for the last minute of the game. Keep it consistent. Go out there and do what your team has practiced, and what you all believe you have the ability to do.

Unsung
and Under
the Radar

· MAX McGEE, PACKERS ·

Wide receiver Max McGee caught 7 passes for 138 yards and 2 touchdowns in Super Bowl I. He was an unlikely hero for the Green Bay Packers in their 35-10 victory over the Kansas City Chiefs. The 34-year-old McGee, who had caught only four passes that season, did not expect to play in the Super Bowl. He was pressed into duty after Boyd Dowler suffered a shoulder injury in the first quarter.

"Max wasn't even thinking about playing.
In fact, he didn't even bring his helmet to the game, didn't have a helmet in his travel bag. After we got back from dinner the night before, Max said, 'Come on, let's go back out.' I said, 'No, I'm staying in. You can do what you want to do.'

Hawg Hanner came in and took check. I remember Max saying, 'Hawg, you gonna double check?' Hawg had been one of our teammates, and he said, 'No, I'm not gonna double check. You're too old to go out anyway.' Max went out, and he was out all night. Came in at 8.

We were sitting on the bench together, and Dowler got hurt in the first quarter. Lombardi instinctively hollered for McGee. Somebody else had been playing in front of McGee at that time. Might have been Bob Long. But instead of hollering for Long, he hollered for McGee. So McGee looks around, and he borrows a helmet from one of the linemen, I think. It didn't fit right.

Max came back after the first series. He sat down by me, and he made the statement:
'You know, if Bart Starr throws me the football, I'll win the car,'
meaning the MVP of the first Super Bowl."

PAUL HORNUNG, *running back, Packers*

• MATT SNELL AND GEORGE SAUER, JETS •

Quarterback Joe Namath guaranteed victory for the New York Jets in Super Bowl III, and the team delivered, beating the Baltimore Colts, 16-7, in what was considered a monumental upset. Namath was selected the game's MVP. Running back Matt Snell and wide receiver George Sauer were equally deserving of the award. Snell rushed 30 times for 121 yards and the Jets' touchdown. Sauer caught 8 passes of Namath's 17 completions for 133 yards, including 6 for first downs.

"Over the years, I had various people say to me,

'You should've been the MVP of the game.'

I think I may have been overlooked. But you gotta realize when you play on a team with a personality like Joe Namath, the voting is probably going to go his way. I guess [Jets owner] Sonny Werblin felt that I deserved some kind of credit, too. Sonny gave me a mint green Cadillac, the Jets' color. A Cadillac El Dorado. My car was better than what Joe got for being the MVP. That's the way things go sometimes."

MATT SNELL, *running back, Jets*

"Don Maynard had a pulled muscle, but the Colts didn't know about it. They were afraid of him because Don was faster than their defensive backs. They were running zone to his side, with Bobby Boyd short and Jerry Logan covering deep. Don got behind them both on one play early, and Joe Namath was there with the ball. Had Don been well, it would have been a completion, but it was like an inch too long. That was called, by some writer, the most important incomplete pass in pro football history, because it set up the field for us the rest of the day.

We would run to the left and get on the left hash mark—the hash marks then were in a logical position, unlike today, when every play is run basically from the middle of the field. Don would line up on the right side, the wide field, and the Colts would take their zone that way, because they didn't want Don running one-on-one out there with anybody. So I was on the short side, on the left, and the defense was rotating away, to the wide side. That left me open a lot, and Joe could always find you if you were open."

GEORGE SAUER, *wide receiver, Jets*

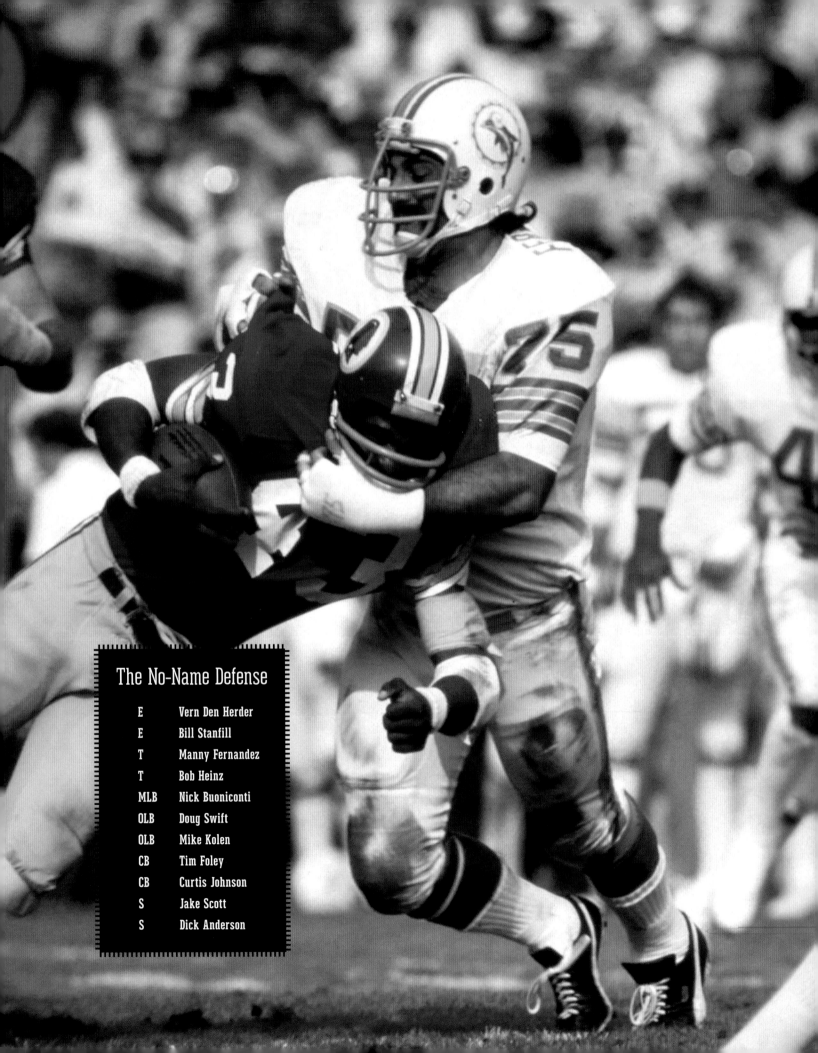

The No-Name Defense

E	Vern Den Herder
E	Bill Stanfill
T	Manny Fernandez
T	Bob Heinz
MLB	Nick Buoniconti
OLB	Doug Swift
OLB	Mike Kolen
CB	Tim Foley
CB	Curtis Johnson
S	Jake Scott
S	Dick Anderson

· MANNY FERNANDEZ, DOLPHINS ·

The Miami Dolphins defeated the Washington Redskins, 14-7, in Super Bowl VII, completing the only unbeaten season in pro football history. The Dolphins went 14-0 in the regular season and 3-0 in the postseason.

Miami's swarming No-Name Defense dominated the game. Safety Jake Scott, who had two interceptions, including one in the end zone to kill a Redskins' drive, was voted the game's most valuable player. The award just as easily could have gone to tackle Manny Fernandez, who was credited with making 17 tackles, at least half of them unassisted.

Fernandez, undersized for his position at 250 pounds, lined up on the center's nose and used his quickness and agility to make plays.

"We got a defensive coach who knew what he was doing—

I think that was the key. Bill Arnsparger came in with a great discipline for a defense that was undisciplined. We had a lot of talent, but we needed some direction. He took freelancing away from guys like myself and Manny Fernandez, got us more structured.

We played a basic defense with a zone behind it.

Bill taught us to understand what other players on the defense were doing. He taught the linebackers to understand what the people behind them were doing.

So we were all on the same page.

We knew what direction we were going in. From there, we started to add to the defense and get a little more sophisticated.

It was a group of people that performed beyond what anybody could have ever expected. It was a chemistry. It was a group of guys who formed a bond on the field and performed like they were protecting the Crown Jewels.

It was just a remarkable group of guys."

NICK BUONICONTI, *linebacker, Dolphins*

• DWIGHT WHITE, STEELERS •

Their famed Steel Curtain defense yielding only 119 yards, including a Super Bowl-low 17 rushing yards, the Pittsburgh Steelers defeated the Minnesota Vikings, 16-6, in Super Bowl IX for the first championship in the franchise's 42-year history.

Steelers defensive end Dwight White spent much of the previous week in a hospital, suffering from a viral infection, but he played most of the game. White accounted for the only scoring in the first half when he sacked Fran Tarkenton in the end zone for a safety—the first points in Steelers' history in a championship game.

"When we got down to New Orleans, Joe Greene and I went out for some dinner in the French Quarter. Before I finished, I had this excruciating pain in my chest and lungs. I guess the most frightening thing was I couldn't breathe—time to be alarmed. Joe literally picked me up, put me in a cab and rushed me back to the hotel. They called the doctor, and later that evening I was in the hospital with viral pneumonia and pleurisy.

That was Saturday night, the week before the game. I think I came out of the hospital on Wednesday and attempted to practice, but I felt too bad and was so weak, and I had to go back in the hospital that same day. I didn't come out until Sunday morning, game day.

I kept telling George Perles, who was the defensive line coach, "Don't worry, Coach, I'll be there." I had lost 20 pounds, and I felt really, really bad. I dressed, and Joe and I went out for some warm-ups. I think Chuck Noll was off on the side, watching me to see how I would do. I found out later they said, "We'll just humor him. We'll let him go through warm-ups. He'll probably collapse on the field. Then we won't have to tell him he can't play." As it turned out, I was able to play all but maybe a couple of series.

People ask me, 'How did you do that? Why did you do that?' Well, over all the years that you play in high school and college and professionally, you lie in bed and dream and fantasize about the big game. That was just too much of an event to miss. The mental toughness, I guess, took over.

After the game I came back to the hotel. There was an all-night diner across the street. I saw one of the Pittsburgh sportswriters having a cheeseburger. I had a cheeseburger with him, and then went back to my room and went to sleep. The next day we went back to Pittsburgh, and I went back into the hospital for a week."

DWIGHT WHITE, *defensive end, Steelers*

Dwight White (78), who had checked out of a hospital earlier in the day, and Jack Lambert (58) stopped Minnesota's Dave Osborn during Super Bowl IX.

• CLARENCE DAVIS, RAIDERS •

The Oakland Raiders upended the Minnesota Vikings, 32-14, in Super Bowl XI for their first NFL championship in front of a record Super Bowl crowd of 103,438 in the Rose Bowl, plus 81 million television viewers, the largest audience ever to watch a sporting event.

Wide receiver Fred Biletnikoff, who made four key receptions for 79 yards, was selected the game's MVP. The award also could have gone to running back Clarence Davis, who rushed 16 times for 137 yards, an average of 8.6 yards. Davis, who had been plagued by a knee injury for three years, had runs of 20, 35, 13, 18 and 16 yards.

The Raiders gained 429 yards, a Super Bowl record at the time.

"The only thing that concerned us about the Vikings was that they had lost three other Super Bowls, and we kept thinking,

'They gotta win one, one of these days.' But it wasn't going to be this week.

We knew if we got past their front four, the rest of the guys were not in a big hurry to make a tackle. You could get some pretty long runs, and obviously we did. Clarence Davis had his biggest day as a pro. Art Shell actually contained Jim Marshall to the point that Marshall didn't have any statistics, didn't have a sack, didn't have a tackle. We just controlled the line of scrimmage."

GENE UPSHAW, *offensive line, Raiders*

"Our offensive line just knocked people out of the way. We had three All-Pros up there. Maybe because everyone said we'd run on them, they believed it. They didn't expect us to go wide. That may have been part of it, but basically we just blocked them inside and outside."

CLARENCE DAVIS, *running back, Raiders*

• 49ERS DEFENSE •

Joe Montana played brilliantly, as usual, in the San Francisco 49ers' 38-16 thrashing of the Miami Dolphins in Super Bowl XIX. Montana passed for 331 yards and three touchdowns, and also scored a touchdown. He was selected the game's MVP.

Just as impressive as Montana was the 49ers defense, which limited Dan Marino to just one touchdown pass. During the regular season, Marino had passed for 48 touchdowns—a record until 2004—and 5,084 yards, and he completed 9 of 10 passes for 103 yards in the first quarter of the Super Bowl.

The 49ers had installed a four-man front for the game, and after Marino's early success, defensive coordinator George Seifert made additional adjustments, pulling a linebacker and inserting a fifth defensive back. Cornerbacks Ronnie Lott and Eric Wright, and safeties Dwight Hicks and Carlton Williamson, who all would play in the Pro Bowl a week later, made certain that Marino's day would be one of the most frustrating of his career.

Under intense pressure, Marino completed only 20 of 40 passes in the final three quarters. He was intercepted twice, and the 49ers sacked him a career-high four times—he had been sacked only 13 times in the regular season. The Dolphins did not score in the second half.

"Dan Marino was having a great year.
No one had stopped him, and I can understand why.

The only way to get to Dan was to put pressure on him.

You had a hard time sacking him because he had the fastest delivery of all time.
But with our platooning, by the time we got into the later stages of the game,
we were putting so much pressure on Dan that he was throwing far sooner than he
should have. So his timing was off, and he didn't have near the consistency.
I rest that on the fact that we could platoon defensive linemen, and they were fresh
and putting the heat on Dan all day."

BILL WALSH, *coach, 49ers*

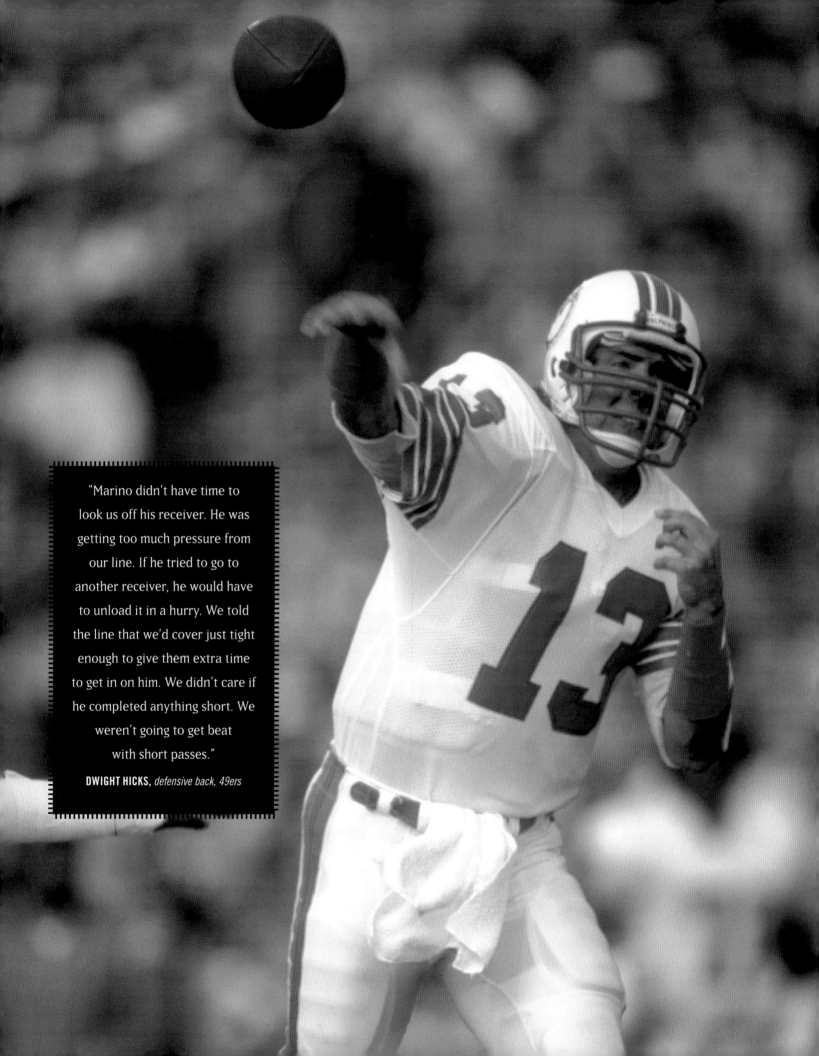

"Marino didn't have time to look us off his receiver. He was getting too much pressure from our line. If he tried to go to another receiver, he would have to unload it in a hurry. We told the line that we'd cover just tight enough to give them extra time to get in on him. We didn't care if he completed anything short. We weren't going to get beat with short passes."

DWIGHT HICKS, *defensive back, 49ers*

"Not taking anything away from Timmy—he made a lot of great runs—but the way our linemen were blocking, I could have picked up 120 yards, and I had a bad leg. One time, they completely wiped out the whole middle of Denver's defensive line. I saw that and I said to myself, 'Oh, my god.'"

DOUG WILLIAMS, *quarterback, Redskins*

• TIMMY SMITH, REDSKINS •

Doug Williams threw four touchdown passes for the Washington Redskins, who overwhelmed the Denver Broncos, 42-10, in Super Bowl XXII. The Redskins set a Super Bowl record for most points in a quarter, 35 in the second period.

Williams, who passed for 340 yards, a Super Bowl record at the time, was selected the game's MVP, but the Redskins had several heroes. Wide receiver Ricky Sanders caught 9 passes for 193 yards, a Super Bowl record at the time. But the most stunning performance came from rookie running back Timmy Smith.

Smith had played in only seven games and rushed for 126 yards during the regular season. He played well in the Redskins two playoff victories, prompting coach Joe Gibbs to put Smith in the starting lineup for the Super Bowl in place of George Rogers.

Smith was faster than Rogers, and the Redskins planned to utilize him on counter plays against the smallish Broncos defense. Smith responded by rushing for 204 yards, a Super Bowl record, and scoring on touchdown runs of 58 and 4 yards.

Smith's time in the spotlight was one of the briefest ever for a Super Bowl hero. He would play in only three seasons—his career ended in 1990—and gain only 944 yards, with 342 coming in postseason games following the 1987 season.

"We ran our counter gap with Timmy. It's the best way to neutralize a quick team like Denver that likes to slant its defense.

They were guessing where we would run, and they guessed right in the first quarter. But they guessed wrong in the second and we got 'em.

We'd get to the hole, and there would be just a linebacker left. All the back had to do was beat a safety, and Timmy had the speed for that."

JOE JACOBY, *offensive lineman, Redskins*

• THURMAN THOMAS, BILLS •

Super Bowl XXV is mainly remembered for Scott Norwood's 47-yard field goal attempt in the final seconds. Make it, and the Buffalo Bills were the NFL champion. The kick sailed wide to the right, and the New York Giants escaped with a 20-19 victory. It was the only Super Bowl among the first 39 decided by one point.

The Giants got superb performances from quarterback Jeff Hostetler, who was an inexperienced second-string player six weeks earlier, and running back Ottis Anderson, whose career had been considered finished four years earlier. Hostetler adeptly executed the Giants' ball-control offense—New York set a Super Bowl record for possession time, 40 minutes, 33 seconds—and passed for 222 yards. Anderson rushed for 102 yards on 21 carries and scored a touchdown.

Anderson was selected the game's MVP, but as he said later, the award almost certainly would have gone to Buffalo running back Thurman Thomas had the Bills won. Thomas touched the ball 20 times and accounted for 190 yards against the Giants' begrudging defense. He rushed 15 times for 135 yards and caught 5 passes for 55 yards.

Thomas ran 31 yards for a touchdown on the opening play of the fourth quarter as the Bills took a 19-17 lead, and he broke a 22-yard run in the Bills' final drive that put Norwood within range of winning the game with a field goal.

It was a signature game for Thomas, who displayed his exceptional versatility as both a runner and a receiver on football's biggest stage.

· LARRY BROWN, COWBOYS ·

The star-studded Dallas Cowboys had an unlikely hero in their 27-17 victory over the Pittsburgh Steelers in Super Bowl XXX. Cornerback Larry Brown, a fifth-year player who had dropped so many interception opportunities earlier in his career that teammate Emmitt Smith nicknamed him Edward Scissorhands, picked off two passes that led to 14 second-half points and helped the Cowboys gain their third Super Bowl victory in four seasons.

Brown became the first cornerback to be selected MVP of the Super Bowl. Five defensive players had previously won the award.

> ### "I just went out and did my job—I didn't look at it that I did anything great.
>
> Neil O'Donnell threw those passes—hey, do you want me to throw them back to him? When people win wars like that, you can't single out people. Larry Brown didn't win that game. Larry Brown needed Troy and Deion and Emmitt and the offensive line and the defensive line. I'm happy that I got noticed, but it's no big deal to me.
>
> The second one, it was a raid, we were going after the quarterback. **I knew that the ball would be thrown quick. They had been running slants on me all day, so I just said, 'I'm gonna go get that one.'** I broke before the receiver broke. I think his timing was off. I don't believe he saw the blitz, but the quarterback did. I went out and got it, and I tried to get to the end zone, but I ran out of gas before I got there."
>
> **LARRY BROWN,** *defensive back, Cowboys*

• DARRIEN GORDON, BRONCOS •

Super Bowl XXXIII was the final game of John Elway's brilliant career, and he went out in unforgettable fashion, leading the Denver Broncos to a 34-19 victory over the Atlanta Falcons for their second consecutive NFL championship.

Elway passed for 336 yards and a touchdown, and the 38-year-old quarterback also became the oldest player to score a touchdown in the Super Bowl when he ran three yards into the end zone.

While Elway reaffirmed his stature as one of pro football's greatest players ever, the Denver secondary also proved that it was not nearly as vulnerable as pre-Super Bowl scouting reports had indicated. (The Broncos had ranked 26th in pass defense during the regular season.) Denver's defensive backs were responsible for each of Atlanta's four turnovers, intercepting three passes and forcing a fumble.

The unsung hero of the Denver secondary was cornerback Darrien Gordon, who intercepted two passes and returned them 108 yards. The yardage is a Super Bowl record.

Gordon dashed the Falcons' hopes of a second-half comeback with interceptions on consecutive possessions inside the Denver 20 that stopped drives and set up Denver touchdowns. Gordon returned the first interception, on a tipped pass, 58 yards to the Falcons' 24. He picked off another pass at the Broncos' 2 and returned it 50 yards.

"We had already proved ourselves against Miami;
we blew them out. Against the Jets, we shut them down.
They were still talking about our secondary, about how weak we were.
But we had only given up six points in two playoff games.

I think we felt vindicated."

DARRIEN GORDON, *defensive back, Broncos*

WILLIAMS

Eddie Robinson, who was my coach at Grambling, summed it up best when we were talking the day after I led the Washington Redskins to a 42–10 victory over the Denver Broncos in Super Bowl XXII. Even sweeter than making history as the first African–American quarterback to play in the Super Bowl was that we had won the game and I had thrown four touchdown passes, a Super Bowl record at the time, and was voted the game's MVP?

Coach Robinson put it all in perspective when he looked at me and said, "Man, you don't understand the impact of what you just did. To me, it was like listening on the radio to the Joe Louis–Max Schmeling fight when I was younger. You will not understand this until you get older."

Now that I look back on it, Coach Robinson probably was right, because at that time I did what I thought I was supposed to do, and everybody would have loved to do: play in the Super Bowl and win the Super Bowl. As time has gone

on, I've run across many people that talk about what that game meant to them, especially to African-Americans, but to people in general.

A lot of people watched what I went through as a quarterback for the Tampa Bay Buccaneers and with the Oklahoma Outlaws of the United States Football League, and even in Washington. A lot of people were pulling for Doug Williams to overcome and to be the first African-American quarterback to play in the Super Bowl.

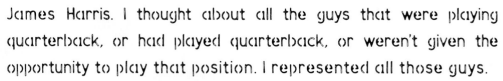

I had to look back at a lot of guys. I thought about Joe Gilliam and James Harris. I thought about all the guys that were playing quarterback, or had played quarterback, or weren't given the opportunity to play that position. I represented all those guys.

The way I viewed it, this wasn't about being black. It was about being the Washington Redskins' quarterback who happened to be black, which was out of my hands. I couldn't buy into all of the hype about a black quarterback and lose focus on what I was in San Diego for, which was to help the Redskins beat the Broncos for the world championship.

The week before the Super Bowl, the NFL makes it mandatory that you appear at three press conferences. I had made up my mind that I was going to give the press exactly what I was supposed to give them, and no more. Unlike a lot of my teammates, I didn't go out and have dinner early in the week. I stayed in the room because there were so many people lurking around the hotel with microphones and tape recorders, trying to get a sound byte.

That week of practice was the best I had ever been involved in because there was so much focus. While everyone else was talking about me being the first black quarterback to play in the game and the matchup with John Elway, we were trying to figure out how we were going to beat the Denver Broncos, not John Elway. I thought, pound for pound, we had the best team. If I were as cocky as Joe Namath was, I would have gone out on the line and guaranteed it.

The Saturday morning before the Super Bowl, I woke up with excruciating pain in my mouth, which led to my undergoing a four-hour root canal. I stayed up that night and watched TV, and the next morning I felt no pain.

That is, until late in the first quarter. After we fell behind 10-0, I hyper-extended my left knee. The trainers came on the field, and I told them, "Don't touch me!" I wanted to know if I could get up on my own. If I could, I knew I was going to be able to finish the game. It was important for me to finish, not only for black America and my family, but also for me being in the Super Bowl. Sure enough, I got up on my own and walked off the field.

Jay Schroeder went in for two plays. He got sacked on the first one, threw an incomplete pass, and then we had to punt. We held Denver, and got the ball back in the second quarter. Our coach, Joe Gibbs, asked me if I was ready to go. I said I was. Then he walked to the bench and told the offensive linemen, "Hey, guys, we're going to get this sucker to rolling."

The first play was a "Charlie-10 Hitch." We faked the fullback up the middle, and if the cornerback played off, the receiver would run a hitch. But if the cornerback pressed, then the receiver would convert it to an up route. Mark Haynes came up to press Ricky Sanders and missed him. Ricky got behind Haynes, and we connected on an 80-yard touchdown pass. We would go on to score on our next four possessions, three of which ended with me throwing touchdown passes, to build a 35-10 halftime lead.

At halftime, I got a painkilling shot in my knee. Joe Bugel, our offensive coordinator, walked up to me and said, "Stud, you don't have to finish this if you don't want to. I think we can handle it from here." I told him, "Coach, I started this game; I'm going to finish this one."

Toward the end of the game, our left tackle, Joe Jacoby, walked up to me and said, "Green, black, yellow, whatever. All I want you to know is you're our quarterback."

Greatest
Show on Earth

The majesty of the Super Bowl: Fighter jets soared in formation over San Diego's Qualcomm Stadium prior to XXXII; Vanessa Williams sang the National Anthem for XXX at Tempe, Arizona; Al Hirt performed during pregame festivities prior to I at Los Angeles.

The Cincinnati Bengals stood at attention on the Pontiac Silverdome sideline moments before Super Bowl XVI, ready to play the San Francisco 49ers. All that remained before kickoff was the National Anthem, to be performed by one of Motown's royalty.

"I had never seen a celebrity in my life," says Cris Collinsworth, then a rookie wide receiver for the Bengals. "Diana Ross comes walking slowly right down our line of players, and she was gorgeous, just gorgeous. We're all looking at her, and you can see one guy's mouth after another fall open as she comes walking down the line.

"I still think that's the reason we started off so poorly in that game."

The Bengals fell behind, 20-0, in the first half before

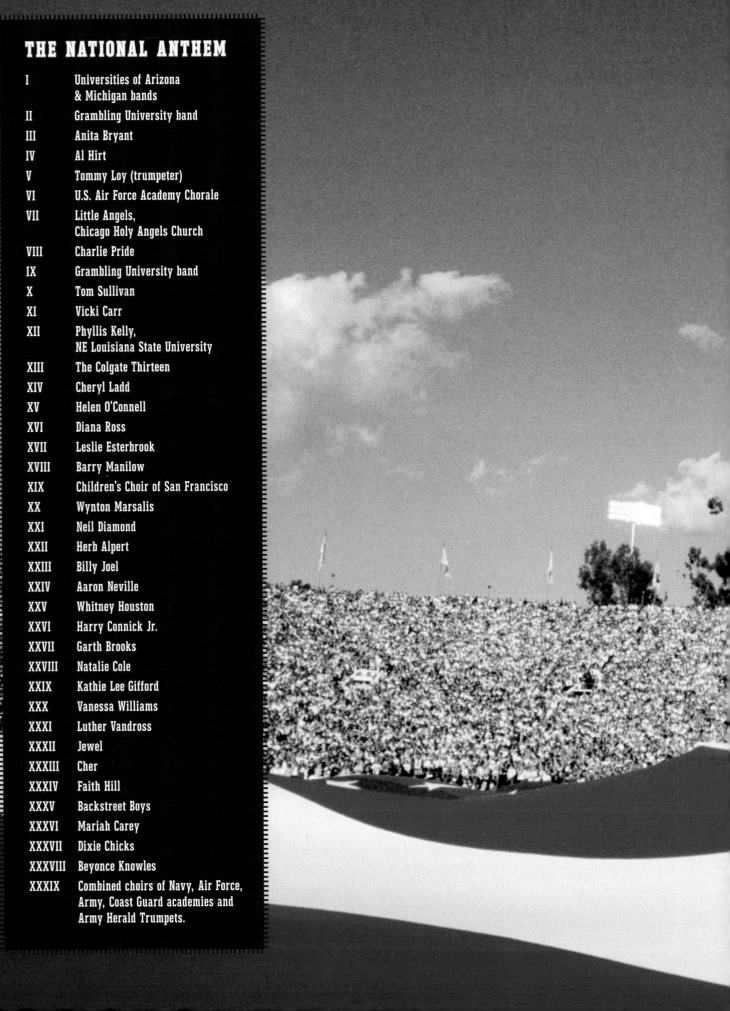

THE NATIONAL ANTHEM

I	Universities of Arizona & Michigan bands
II	Grambling University band
III	Anita Bryant
IV	Al Hirt
V	Tommy Loy (trumpeter)
VI	U.S. Air Force Academy Chorale
VII	Little Angels, Chicago Holy Angels Church
VIII	Charlie Pride
IX	Grambling University band
X	Tom Sullivan
XI	Vicki Carr
XII	Phyllis Kelly, NE Louisiana State University
XIII	The Colgate Thirteen
XIV	Cheryl Ladd
XV	Helen O'Connell
XVI	Diana Ross
XVII	Leslie Esterbrook
XVIII	Barry Manilow
XIX	Children's Choir of San Francisco
XX	Wynton Marsalis
XXI	Neil Diamond
XXII	Herb Alpert
XXIII	Billy Joel
XXIV	Aaron Neville
XXV	Whitney Houston
XXVI	Harry Connick Jr.
XXVII	Garth Brooks
XXVIII	Natalie Cole
XXIX	Kathie Lee Gifford
XXX	Vanessa Williams
XXXI	Luther Vandross
XXXII	Jewel
XXXIII	Cher
XXXIV	Faith Hill
XXXV	Backstreet Boys
XXXVI	Mariah Carey
XXXVII	Dixie Chicks
XXXVIII	Beyonce Knowles
XXXIX	Combined choirs of Navy, Air Force, Army, Coast Guard academies and Army Herald Trumpets.

Surrounded by a crowd of more than 98,000 in the Rose Bowl,
Garth Brooks sang the National Anthem for Super Bowl XXVII.
Marlee Matlin provided the American Sign Language performance.

James Brown at halftime in XXXI at New Orleans; Steven Tyler of Aerosmith and Britney Spears at halftime in XXXV at Tampa; Apollo 8 astronauts Frank Borman, James Lovell and William Anders led the crowd in the Pledge of Allegiance before III at Miami.

clawing back in the second half, only to lose, 26-21. "If she'd have walked down the 49ers sideline," Collinsworth says, perhaps only half-joking, "maybe we'd have won that game."

Ross' role in the game's outcome notwithstanding, her appearance on January 24, 1982 was a watershed moment in Super Bowl history. She was easily the biggest celebrity involved in the pregame or halftime festivities at that time. Since then, the NFL has adopted Ross' mantra:

Ain't no mountain high enough. The roster of Super Bowl performers now includes Michael Jackson, James Brown, Garth Brooks, Cher, Stevie Wonder, Sting, Aerosmith, *NSYNC, Shania Twain, U2 and Paul McCartney.

Celebrity performances represent an affirmation of Pete Rozelle and Paul Tagliabue's Super Bowl mission statements. Rozelle, the late NFL commissioner who presided over the birth of the game and shaped its evolution for three decades,

Shania Twain at halftime in XXXVII at San Diego.

THE HALFTIME ENTERTAINMENT

	TALENT
I	Universities of Arizona & Michigan bands
II	Grambling University band
III	Florida A&M band
IV	Carol Channing
V	Florida A&M band
VI	Ella Fitzgerald, Carol Channing, Al Hirt, U.S. Marine Corps Drill Team
VII	University of Michigan band, Woody Herman
VIII	University of Texas band
IX	Mercer Ellington and Grambling University bands
X	Up With People
XI	Los Angeles Unified all-city band and crowd participation
XII	Tyler Apache Belles, Pete Fountain, Al Hirt
XIII	Ken Hamilton, various Caribbean bands
XIV	Up With People
XV	Southern University band, Helen O'Connell
XVI	Up With People
XVII	Los Angeles Super Drill Team
XVIII	University of Florida and Florida State University bands
XIX	U.S. Air Force Band: "Tops in Blue"
XX	Up With People
XXI	Southern California-area high school drill teams and dancers
XXII	Chubby Checker/Rockettes & 88 grand pianos
XXIII	South Florida-area dancers and performers and 3-D effects
XXIV	Pete Fountain, Doug Kershaw, Irma Thomas
XXV	New Kids on the Block
XXVI	Gloria Estefan, Brian Boitano, Dorothy Hamill
XXVII	Michael Jackson
XXVIII	Clint Black, Tanya Tucker, Travis Tritt, Wynonna and Naomi Judd
XXIX	Patti LaBelle, Tony Bennett, Arturo Sandoval, Miami Sound Machine
XXX	Diana Ross
XXXI	Blues Brothers: Dan Akroyd, John Goodman, James Belushi; ZZ Top, James Brown
XXXII	Boyz II Men, Smokey Robinson, Martha Reeves, Temptations, Queen Latifah
XXXIII	Stevie Wonder, Gloria Estefan, Big Bad Voodoo Daddy, tap dancer Savion Glover
XXXIV	Phil Collins, Christina Aguilera, Enrique Iglesias, Toni Braxton, 80-person choir
XXXV	Aerosmith and *NSYNC
XXXVI	U2
XXXVII	Shania Twain
XXXVIII	Janet Jackson
XXXIX	Paul McCartney

*(top to bottom) Al Hirt, VI, New Orleans; Tony Bennett, XXIX, Miami; Queen Latifah, XXXII, San Diego; Michael Jackson, XXVII, Pasadena, CA; ZZ Top, XXXI, New Orleans; Naomi and Wynonna Judd, XXVIII, Atlanta; *NSYNC, XXXV, Tampa*

For players, the Super Bowl experience includes mass meetings with media from all corners of the world. Philadelphia Eagles quarterback Donovan McNabb dutifully obliged during the week prior to Super Bowl XXXIX at Jacksonville.

pounded his philosophy into the hearts and minds of his NFL staff: The Super Bowl must be an experience that people will remember for the rest of their lives. Tagliabue, who replaced Rozelle in 1989, embraced that foundation and built on it.

The players and coaches do their part to make that a reality through competition at its highest level. But so much more has gone into making the Super Bowl what it is today. Even before it was called the Super Bowl, "super"

From the start, Rozelle made some groundbreaking moves that would impact the growth of the game. He decided that the first meeting between the AFL and NFL champions would take place two weeks after the respective league title games. That way, the media had more time to hype the game. At the same time, Rozelle blew out the budget to both accommodate and entertain media covering the game. "Make it an event the media will want to cover every year," he said. Today, more than 3,000 media

was the name of the game. Rozelle had a public relations background before rising to commissioner, and PR pros are always taught to think big. It didn't hurt that Rozelle had a little P.T. Barnum in him, as well. He may not have dreamed the Super Bowl would become the "Greatest Show on Earth"—but he did, in fact, do everything in his power to make that happen.

credentials are issued for the Super Bowl, and no expense is spared on private parties thrown for the media and other NFL associates during Super Bowl week.

Did someone say party? The concept of "Super Bowl party" takes on a very different meaning depending on whether you are a corporate or celebrity insider attending the game, or simply one of millions of fans watching the

THE NFL EXPERIENCE

Children and adults alike enjoy the NFL Experience in the host city during Super Bowl week. The NFL Experience, which was launched in 1992, is an interactive theme park offering participatory games, displays and entertainment attractions. Pictured here are scenes from the NFL Experience in San Diego in 2003 and Houston in 2004.

*Arizona Cardinals owner Bill Bidwell (holding a
football helmet) and former Cardinals Community
Relations director Adele Harris (center), for whom
the facility was named, were among the dignitaries
at the dedication of the Phoenix YET Center prior
to Super Bowl XXX.*

game in living rooms and bars around the
world.

The origin of the posh Super Bowl party
dates to January 1973, when Rozelle hosted
a big bash on board the Queen Mary, which
was docked in Long Beach, California. The
Commissioner's Party is now an annual
event on the Friday night before Super
Sunday, a lavish affair for more than 3,000
invited guests.

If you can't make the Friday night party,
there's always the Saturday afternoon
gathering hosted by agent Leigh Steinberg
and attended by celebrities, politicians and
star athletes. Steinberg has held his bash
in prominent locales such as the San Diego
Zoo, Sea World in Miami and Busch
Gardens in Tampa. But pace yourself,
because Saturday night features even
more private parties, hosted by Playboy

Football fans spend more than

$50,000,000

on food during the four days of the Super Bowl weekend.

Enterprises, *Maxim* magazine and various high-profile NFL corporate partners. For some parties invitations are harder to come by than Super Bowl tickets.

Parties and football games aren't the only places where money is thrown around. Tagliabue's focus has always been the "twin pillars of football and community." Nowhere has that been more apparent than in the Super Bowl host cities, from

The Super Bowl can have a lasting impact on countless youth through the NFL's Youth Education Town initiative. The program provides for the construction of educational and recreational centers for youth in at-risk neighborhoods in Super Bowl host cities. (Above) Children enjoy the YET Center in Tampa, which opened in 2003. Under commissioner Paul Tagliabue (opposite, bottom), the NFL donates $1 million annually to the YET initiative.

the standpoint of both economic and charitable development.

"Under Paul Tagliabue's direction, we came to understand that the Super Bowl was about much more than the game for the people in the host city," said Jim Steeg, who ran the NFL's Super Bowl operations from 1980 to 2005. Every year since 1993, the NFL has broken ground on a Youth Education Town in the host city

Frito-Lay, the nation's largest chip manufacturer, increases production in the weeks leading up to the Super Bowl by more than

10,000,000 pounds.

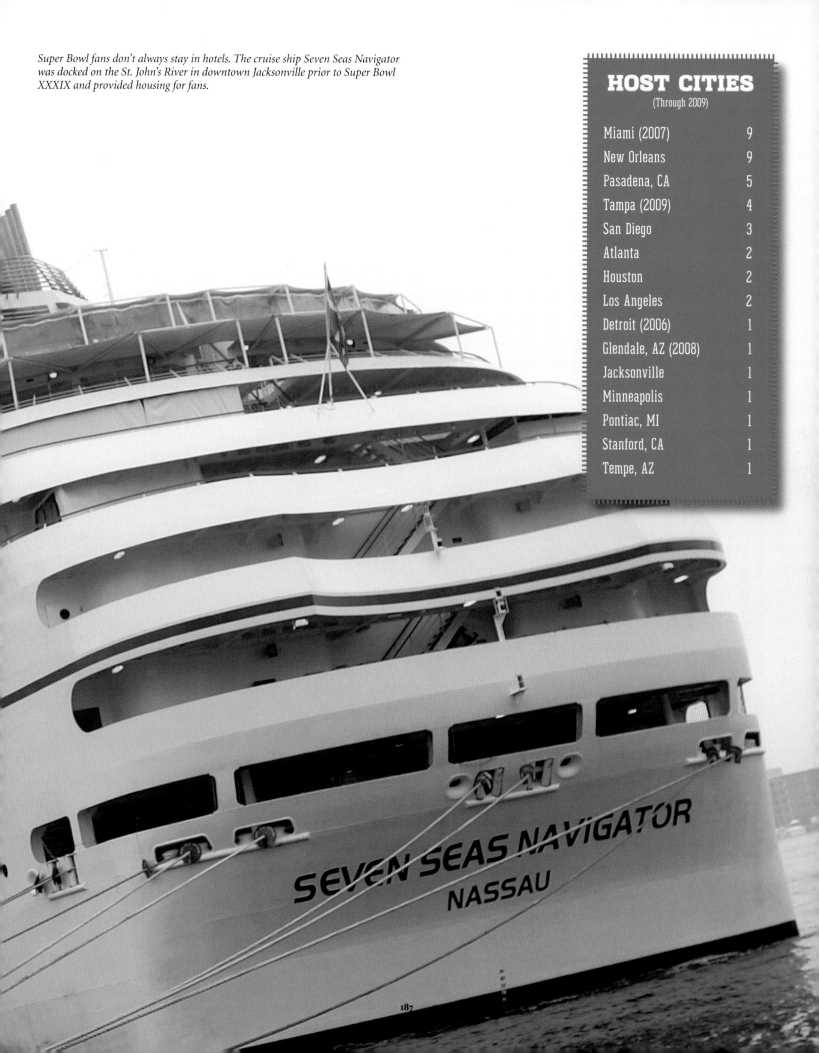

Super Bowl fans don't always stay in hotels. The cruise ship *Seven Seas Navigator* was docked on the St. John's River in downtown Jacksonville prior to Super Bowl XXXIX and provided housing for fans.

HOST CITIES
(Through 2009)

Miami (2007)	9
New Orleans	9
Pasadena, CA	5
Tampa (2009)	4
San Diego	3
Atlanta	2
Houston	2
Los Angeles	2
Detroit (2006)	1
Glendale, AZ (2008)	1
Jacksonville	1
Minneapolis	1
Pontiac, MI	1
Stanford, CA	1
Tempe, AZ	1

—educational and recreational centers aimed at positively impacting youth from at-risk neighborhoods. "To me, the most important thing we did was the YET centers; the fact that we left a permanent legacy of the Super Bowl," Steeg says.

the country and the world. The foundation for these parties can be found not in the Super Bowl's star power, but rather in the tradition of tailgating and football's propensity for bringing families and groups together for merriment and celebration around a game. The cumulative impact of

A view from Jacksonville's Alltel Stadium at the festivities below before the start of Super Bowl XXXIX between the New England Patriots and the Philadelphia Eagles.

That legacy can also be measured in the overall economic impact to the Super Bowl host city, easily more than $100 million each year, not to mention the positive exposure from a tourism angle. It's no wonder the competition for playing host to the Super Bowl is as fierce as the competition to play in them.

Far less formal than NFL-associated parties in the host city are the Super Bowl parties and gatherings held around

Super Bowl parties around the country is nothing short of staggering.

For instance, the top-selling Super Bowl-licensed products each year are not hats or jerseys or T-shirts, but rather napkins and paper plates and plastic cups. According to *The Wall Street Journal*, "The Super Bowl has become America's biggest excuse for having a party, surpassing even New Year's Eve."

As football images flashed in the background, Ricky Martin performed at his Super Bowl Saturday Night Party in 2001 at Tampa.

Former Presidents Bill Clinton and George H.W. Bush participated in ceremonies before Super Bowl XXXIX. They appeared on Fox TV's pregame show and pled for support of tsunami victims.

"My memories of going to the White House after we won the Super Bowl, well, first thing,

Bush was taller than I thought he was;

and he didn't look as wimpy as everybody said he was. My wife, Patricia, was just in awe of
everything. We were in this room, and it's got all these treasures everywhere. I'm standing there
with Patricia, and Mr. and Mrs. Bush. My wife wants to say something, but she doesn't know what to say.
She turns to Mrs. Bush and she goes, 'You have a really nice house here.' Like, 'Gee, Ethel,
nice place.' She looked at me, and she got this look like, 'Did I just say that?' And we just
kind of chuckled. So now I always mess with her: 'Gee, Mrs. Bush. Nice house.' "

MATT MILLEN, *linebacker, 49ers*

Tailgate parties are part of Super Bowl tradition. Baltimore Ravens fans engaged in the ritual prior to XXXV at Tampa, and Cincinnati Bengals and San Francisco 49ers fans alike enjoyed the MTV tailgate bash before XXIII at Miami. (Bottom) Back home in New York, Giants fans filled a saloon and rooted for their team against the Ravens in XXXV.

The paper goods industry is not the only group to benefit. According to various reports, Super Sunday trails only Thanksgiving Day for food consumption in America. It is the biggest sales day of the year for Domino's Pizza. The California Avocado Commission says that nearly 40 million pounds of avocados are eaten during Super Bowl festivities, and that more guacamole is consumed on Super Sunday than on any other days of the year except Memorial Day and Cinco de Mayo. Super Bowl week is also the busiest time of year for television sales, especially large-screen TVs. However, there are few statistics during Super Bowl week. Not suprisingly, there are fewer weddings on Super Sunday than on any other day of the year.

The lasting memories that Rozelle envisioned have also come in the form of TV commercials. A year after Diana Ross brought star power to the National Anthem in Super Bowl

A yellow bow 80 feet long and 30 feet wide hung over the main entrance of the Louisiana Superdome for Super Bowl XV, and 80,000 miniature bows were distributed to those attending the game. The bows commemorated the release of 52 Americans who had been held hostage for 444 days after Iranians took over the United States embassy in Tehran. The group had been taken to Germany, where each received a copy of the Super Bowl program, courtesy of NFL commissioner Pete Rozelle, who anticipated they would want to watch the game on television.

XVII, Apple unofficially launched the Super Bowl ad wars with the 1984 spot introducing the Macintosh computer. Madison Avenue has since followed Rozelle's "think big" philosophy, to the point that Super Bowl commercials rival the game itself as a Monday morning topic of conversation. A 30-second spot during the game cost $2 million in 2003, and the rate increases each year.

Whether you are at the game or

watching at home, you can't deny that the images and emotions both on and off the field have made an indelible mark on American culture. Some of the indelible memories:

• The giant yellow ribbon draped around the Louisiana Superdome for Super Bowl XV, honoring the hostages who were freed from Iran just days before the game.

• Whitney Houston's stirring rendition

Fighter jets soared over the Rose Bowl before Super Bowl XXVII.
Whitney Houston sang the National Anthem for XXV at Tampa.

of the National Anthem at Super Bowl XXV in 1991, while American troops were engaged in Operation Desert Storm in the Middle East.

• Budweiser frogs and Pepsi dancing bears.

• The power and majesty of military jets flying over the stadium.

• The pyrotechnics of a pregame performance from the legendary rock band KISS.

• The first Super Bowl following the terrorist attacks on the World Trade Center. U2 electrified a worldwide audience, performing while the names of the 9-11 victims scrolled in the background.

"It's amazing," U2 leader Bono said a few days before his performance at Super Bowl XXXVI. "To be here at the Super Bowl, to know this is the very heart of America … it feels right."

The halftime show of Super Bowl XXXVI at New Orleans was a tribute to those who died in the 9/11 terrorist attacks. Bono, of the Irish rock group U2, not only performed, but also displayed his affection for America.

STAUBACH

With the times we're going through now, the Super Bowl is a great diversion because it's something that so many people look forward to. Unlike other major sporting events, such as the World Series or the NBA Finals or the Masters, it's a one-day deal. You crown the champion that day.

And those other events aren't watched like the Super Bowl.

There are guys with wives and girlfriends who couldn't care less about football, but they still know about the Super Bowl. Although my wife watched me play for a long time and will go to Cowboys games with me, I wouldn't say she is really big into football. But she'll sit there and watch the whole Super Bowl.

Even though it's kind of a corporate-type event now, it's still people in these corporations that are going to the game. You look at the ticket prices, and they've gone out of sight. They could probably charge $5,000 for a ticket, and they'd still sell the place out—that's how great the demand is. And the demand just continues to get bigger and bigger. You wonder how much bigger it can get, but the amazing thing is that it probably still has some room to grow.

People watch a lot of TV. They watch some crazy, loony, reality—based shows. But the one consistent programming they watch is football because they relate to it. And the Super Bowl's the biggest reason for that. It all leads to the Super Bowl.

So many things in the business and entertainment worlds are positioned around the Super Bowl. Companies base their incentive programs around the game. I go to business meetings, and without fail somebody will ask me, "Who's going to win the Super Bowl this year?"

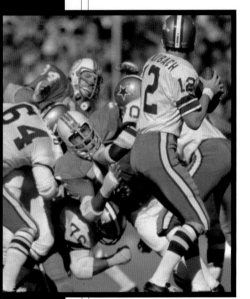

The season hasn't started yet, but that's the sort of anticipation that you have. I still have it. And a lot of that has to do with the content that the Super Bowl provides to television. It's a real driver.

Growing up in Cincinnati, Ohio, in the 1950s, I started to see that the NFL was having some success on TV, and it really started to take off in the late 1950s. Then came the NFL's merger with the AFL. In 1969, when I joined the Cowboys from the Naval Academy, I kind of got in when the league was really on a roll.

It was the Vietnam era. There were a lot of things that were taking place in the country and around the world. And the Super Bowl and football became an outpouring of being involved in something they could all share.

People still ask me today what playing in the Super Bowl was like. We played in the Superdome in New Orleans for Super Bowl XII—we beat Denver, 27–10— and it was overwhelming. You couldn't hear anything because it was indoors and people were screaming. Everyone was nervous. I remember our running back, Robert Newhouse, saying to me, "Maybe you've got to get these guys under control."

"Hey, Robert," I said. "I'm trying to get myself under control."

But you react on what you do, the repetition in practice. You move yourself back into the zone of competition, whether it's the Super Bowl or another game. Early on, it's the hardest thing to get to the point where you're executing the way you want and doing the things that you know you can do. One of the important qualities of an athlete is to perform at your highest level when the pressure is on. Some guys do and some don't. And sometimes your highest level is not enough when the pressure is on.

I'm grateful for my NFL career, and I'm totally grateful to the Naval Academy. Even though I was only in the service for four years—including active duty in Vietnam—I really felt very close to the military, especially to the Navy and the Marine Corps because of my time in the Naval Academy.

When I was introduced before a game as, "Roger Staubach, Navy," I was really proud of that. I've had a common denominator with a lot of great military people because I went to the Naval Academy and was in the service. My heroes had been guys that have devoted their lives to the service. We had 14 or 15 admirals from our class at the Academy. We've got a number of former admirals who work for The Staubach Company, a global real estate advisory firm. The Navy is still a big part of our life.

I played in cities where most of the fans probably hated the Cowboys, but there were enough service people there that probably didn't hate me. I got a very warm feeling in a lot of the cities we were in because I think they related to me, as far as being someone that was in the service.

I appreciate the strong link that has developed through the years between the NFL and the United States military. The Super Bowl has had a lot to do with that bond because each year it is surrounded by a major celebration of patriotism. It has been a very positive thing.

It's a wonderful outlet that we have.

For the
Record

SUPER BOWL RESULTS

No.	Date	Site	Result	MVP
I	January 15, 1967	Los Angeles	Green Bay 35, Kansas City 10	Bart Starr, qb
II	January 14, 1968	Miami	Green Bay 33, Oakland 14	Bart Starr, qb
III	January 12, 1969	Miami	New York Jets 16, Baltimore 7	Joe Namath, qb
IV	January 11, 1970	New Orleans	Kansas City 23, Minnesota 7	Len Dawson, qb
V	January 17, 1971	Miami	Baltimore 16, Dallas 13	Chuck Howley, lb
VI	January 16, 1972	New Orleans	Dallas 24, Miami 3	Roger Staubach, qb
VII	January 14, 1973	Los Angeles	Miami 14, Washington 7	Jake Scott, s
VIII	January 13, 1974	Houston	Miami 24, Minnesota 7	Larry Csonka, rb
IX	January 12, 1975	New Orleans	Pittsburgh 16, Minnesota 6	Franco Harris, rb
X	January 18, 1976	Miami	Pittsburgh 21, Dallas 17	Lynn Swann, wr
XI	January 9, 1977	Pasadena, CA	Oakland 32, Minnesota 14	Fred Biletnikoff, wr
XII	January 15, 1978	New Orleans	Dallas 27, Denver 10	Randy White, dt; Harvey Martin, de
XIII	January 21, 1979	Miami	Pittsburgh 35, Dallas 31	Terry Bradshaw, qb
XIV	January 20, 1980	Pasadena, CA	Pittsburgh 31, Los Angeles Rams 19	Terry Bradshaw, qb
XV	January 25, 1981	New Orleans	Oakland 27, Philadelphia 10	Jim Plunkett, qb
XVI	January 24, 1982	Pontiac, MI	San Francisco 26, Cincinnati 21	Joe Montana, qb
XVII	January 30, 1983	Pasadena, CA	Washington 27, Miami 17	John Riggins, rb
XVIII	January 22, 1984	Tampa	Los Angeles Raiders 38, Washington 9	Marcus Allen, rb
XIX	January 20, 1985	Stanford, CA	San Francisco 38, Miami 16	Joe Montana, qb
XX	January 26, 1986	New Orleans	Chicago 46, New England 10	Richard Dent, de
XXI	January 25, 1987	Pasadena, CA	New York Giants 39, Denver 20	Phil Simms, qb
XXII	January 31, 1988	San Diego	Washington 42, Denver 10	Doug Williams, qb
XXIII	January 22, 1989	Miami	San Francisco 20, Cincinnati 16	Jerry Rice, wr
XXIV	January 28, 1990	New Orleans	San Francisco 55, Denver 10	Joe Montana, qb
XXV	January 27, 1991	Tampa	New York Giants 20, Buffalo 19	Ottis Anderson, rb
XXVI	January 26, 1992	Minneapolis	Washington 37, Buffalo 24	Mark Rypien, qb
XXVII	January 31, 1993	Pasadena, CA	Dallas 52, Buffalo 17	Troy Aikman, qb
XXVIII	January 30, 1994	Atlanta	Dallas 30, Buffalo 13	Emmitt Smith, rb
XXIX	January 29, 1995	Miami	San Francisco 49, San Diego 26	Steve Young, qb
XXX	January 28, 1996	Tempe, AZ	Dallas 27, Pittsburgh 17	Larry Brown, cb
XXXI	January 26, 1997	New Orleans	Green Bay 35, New England 21	Desmond Howard, kr
XXXII	January 25, 1998	San Diego	Denver 31, Green Bay 24	Terrell Davis, rb
XXXIII	January 31, 1999	Miami	Denver 34, Atlanta 19	John Elway, qb
XXXIV	January 30, 2000	Atlanta	St. Louis 23, Tennessee 16	Kurt Warner, qb
XXXV	January 28, 2001	Tampa	Baltimore 34, New York Giants 7	Ray Lewis, lb
XXXVI	February 3, 2002	New Orleans	New England 20, St. Louis 17	Tom Brady, qb
XXXVII	January 26, 2003	San Diego	Tampa Bay 48, Oakland 21	Dexter Jackson, s
XXXVIII	February 1, 2004	Houston	New England 32, Carolina 29	Tom Brady, qb
XXXIX	February 6, 2005	Jacksonville	New England 24, Philadelphia 21	Deion Branch, wr

All MVPs except Chuck Howley played for winning team

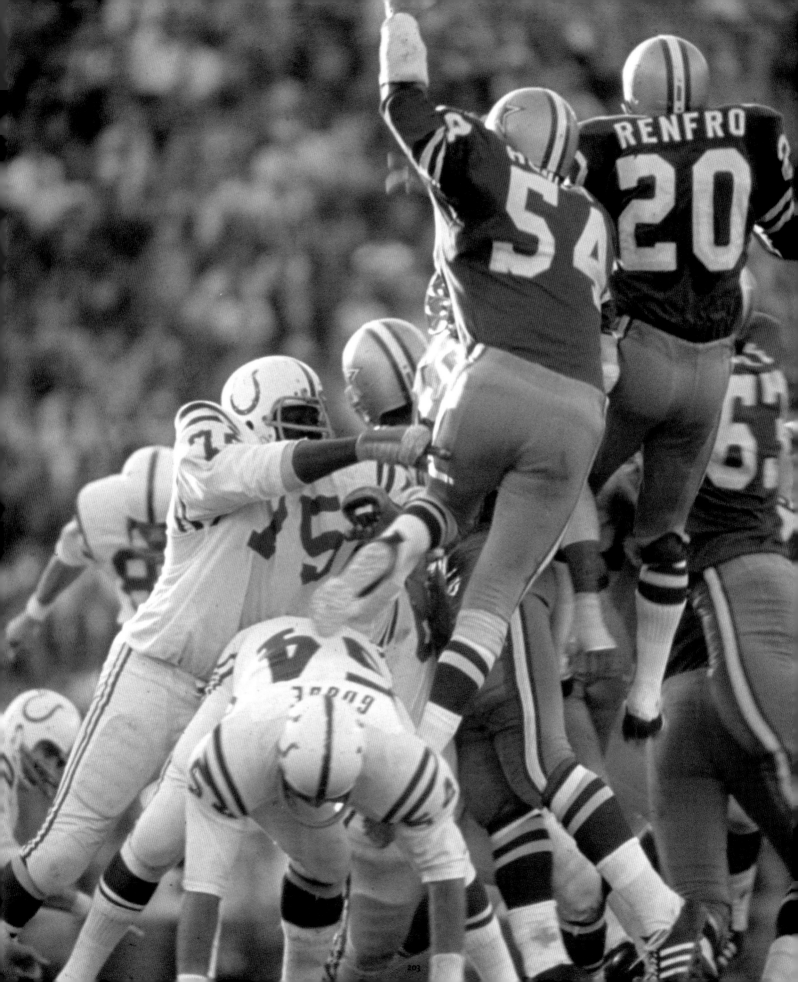

PARTICIPATION: PLAYERS

Games	
6	Mike Lodish, Buffalo, XXV-XXVIII; Denver, XXXII-XXXIII
5	Marv Fleming, Green Bay, I-II; Miami, VI-VIII
5	Larry Cole, Dallas, V-VI, X, XII-XIII
5	Cliff Harris, Dallas, V-VI, X, XII-XIII
5	Charles Haley, San Francisco, XXIII-XXIV; Dallas, XXVII-XXVIII, XXX
5	D.D. Lewis, Dallas, V-VI, X, XII-XIII
5	Preston Pearson, Baltimore, III; Pittsburgh, IX; Dallas, X, XII-XIII
5	Charlie Waters, Dallas, V-VI, X, XII-XIII
5	Rayfield Wright, Dallas, V-VI, X, XII-XIII
5	Cornelius Bennett, Buffalo, XXV-XXVIII; Atlanta, XXXIII
5	John Elway, Denver, XXI-XXII, XXIV, XXXII-XXXIII
5	Glenn Parker, Buffalo, XXV-XXVIII; N.Y. Giants, XXXV
5	Bill Romanowski, San Francisco, XXIII-XXIV; Denver, XXXII-XXXIII; Oakland, XXXVII

Winning Team	
5	Charles Haley, San Francisco, XXIII-XXIV; Dallas, XXVII-XXVIII, XXX

Mike Lodish

COACHES

Games	
6	Don Shula, Baltimore, III; Miami, VI-VIII, XVII, XIX
5	Tom Landry, Dallas, V-VI, X, XII-XIII
4	Bud Grant, Minnesota, IV, VIII-IX, XI
4	Chuck Noll, Pittsburgh, IX-X, XIII-XIV
4	Joe Gibbs, Washington, XVII-XVIII, XXII, XXVI
4	Marv Levy, Buffalo, XXV-XXVIII
4	Dan Reeves, Denver, XXI-XXII, XXIV; Atlanta, XXXIII

Winning Team	
4	Chuck Noll, Pittsburgh, IX-X, XIII-XIV
3	Bill Walsh, San Francisco, XVI, XIX, XXIII
3	Joe Gibbs, Washington, XVII, XXII, XXVI
3	Bill Belichick, New England, XXXVI, XXXVIII-XXXIX

Losing Team	
4	Bud Grant, Minnesota, IV, VIII-IX, XI
4	Don Shula, Baltimore, III; Miami, VI, XVII, XIX
4	Marv Levy, Buffalo, XXV-XXVIII
4	Dan Reeves, Denver, XXI-XXII, XXIV; Atlanta, XXXIII

Don Shula

Charles Haley

SCORING

Points, Career		G	TD
48	Jerry Rice, San Francisco	4	8
30	Emmitt Smith, Dallas	3	5
24	Franco Harris, Pittsburgh	4	4
24	Roger Craig, San Francisco	3	4
24	Thurman Thomas, Buffalo	4	4
24	John Elway, Denver	5	4

Points, Game		SB	TD
18	Roger Craig, San Francisco	XIX	3
18	Jerry Rice, San Francisco	XXIV	3
18	Jerry Rice, San Francisco	XXIX	3
18	Ricky Watters, San Francisco	XXIX	3
18	Terrell Davis, Denver	XXXII	3

DEFENSE

Sacks, Career		G
4.5	Charles Haley, San Francisco-Dallas	5
3.0	Danny Stubbs, San Francisco	2
3.0	Leonard Marshall, N.Y. Giants	2
3.0	Jeff Wright, Buffalo	4
3.0	Reggie White, Green Bay	2
3.0	Willie McGinest, New England	4
3.0	Tedy Bruschi, New England	4
3.0	Mike Vrabel, New England	3

Sacks, Game		SB
3.0	Reggie White, Green Bay	XXXI

Safeties		SB
1	Dwight White, Pittsburgh	IX
1	Reggie Harrison, Pittsburgh	X
1	Henry Waechter, Chicago	XX
1	George Martin, NY Giants	XXI
1	Bruce Smith, Buffalo	XXV

Interceptions, Career		G
3	Chuck Howley, Dallas	2
3	Rod Martin, Oakland-LA Raiders	2
3	Larry Brown, Dallas	3

Interceptions, Game		SB
3	Rod Martin, Oakland	XV

Longest Return		SB
75	Willie Brown, Oakland	XI (TD)
60	Herb Adderley, Green Bay	II (TD)
58	Darrien Gordon, Denver	XXXIII

100 YARD
RUSHERS

	SB	Att	Yds	TD
Timmy Smith, **Washington**	22	22	204	2
Marcus Allen, **LA Raiders**	18	20	191	2
John Riggins, **Washington**	17	38	166	1
Franco Harris, **Pittsburgh**	9	34	158	1
Terrell Davis, **Denver**	32	30	157	3
Larry Csonka, **Miami**	8	33	145	2
Clarence Davis, **Oakland**	11	16	137	0
Thurman Thomas, **Buffalo**	25	15	135	1
Emmitt Smith, **Dallas**	28	30	132	2
Michael Pittman, **Tampa Bay**	37	29	124	0
Matt Snell, **NY Jets**	3	30	121	1
Tom Matte, **Baltimore**	3	11	116	0
Larry Csonka, **Miami**	7	15	112	0
Emmitt Smith, **Dallas**	27	22	108	1
Ottis Anderson, **NY Giants**	25	21	102	1
Terrell Davis, **Denver**	33	25	102	0
Jamal Lewis, **Baltimore**	35	27	102	1

* Super Bowl MVP

100 YARD
RECEIVERS

	SB	C	Yds	TD
* Jerry Rice, San Francisco	23	11	215	1
Ricky Sanders, Washington	22	9	193	2
Isaac Bruce, St. Louis	34	6	162	1
* Lynn Swann, Pittsburgh	10	4	161	1
Andre Reed, Buffalo	27	8	152	0
Rod Smith, Denver	33	5	152	1
Jerry Rice, San Francisco	29	10	149	3
Jerry Rice, San Francisco	24	7	148	3
Deion Branch, New England	38	10	143	1
Muhsin Muhammad, Carolina	38	4	140	1
Max McGee, Green Bay	1	7	138	2
* Deion Branch, New England	39	11	133	0
George Sauer, NY Jets	3	8	133	0
Willie Gault, Chicago	20	4	129	0
Antonio Freeman, Green Bay	32	9	126	2
Lynn Swann, Pittsburgh	13	7	124	1
Terrell Owens, Philadelphia	39	9	122	0
Vance Johnson, Denver	21	5	121	1
John Stallworth, Pittsburgh	14	3	121	1
John Stallworth, Pittsburgh	13	3	115	2
Gary Clark, Washington	26	7	114	1
Michael Irvin, Dallas	27	6	114	2
Art Monk, Washington	26	7	113	0
John Henderson, Minnesota	4	7	111	0
Torry Holt, St. Louis	34	7	109	1
Cris Collinsworth, Cincinnati	16	5	107	0
Antonio Freeman, Green Bay	31	3	105	1
Dan Ross, Cincinnati (te)	16	11	104	2
Roger Craig, San Francisco (rb)	23	8	101	0

* Super Bowl MVP

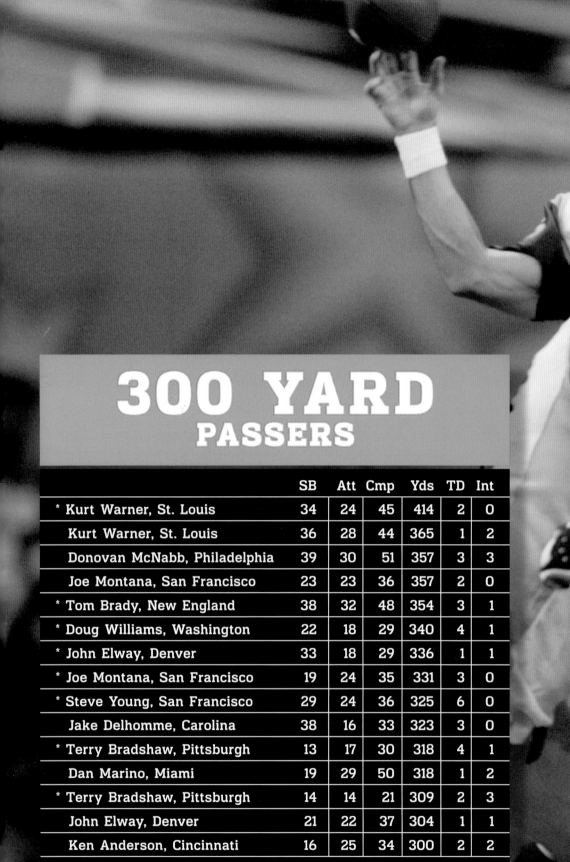

300 YARD
PASSERS

	SB	Att	Cmp	Yds	TD	Int
* Kurt Warner, St. Louis	34	24	45	414	2	0
Kurt Warner, St. Louis	36	28	44	365	1	2
Donovan McNabb, Philadelphia	39	30	51	357	3	3
Joe Montana, San Francisco	23	23	36	357	2	0
* Tom Brady, New England	38	32	48	354	3	1
* Doug Williams, Washington	22	18	29	340	4	1
* John Elway, Denver	33	18	29	336	1	1
* Joe Montana, San Francisco	19	24	35	331	3	0
* Steve Young, San Francisco	29	24	36	325	6	0
Jake Delhomme, Carolina	38	16	33	323	3	0
* Terry Bradshaw, Pittsburgh	13	17	30	318	4	1
Dan Marino, Miami	19	29	50	318	1	2
* Terry Bradshaw, Pittsburgh	14	14	21	309	2	3
John Elway, Denver	21	22	37	304	1	1
Ken Anderson, Cincinnati	16	25	34	300	2	2

* Super Bowl MVP

SUPER BOWL RINGS

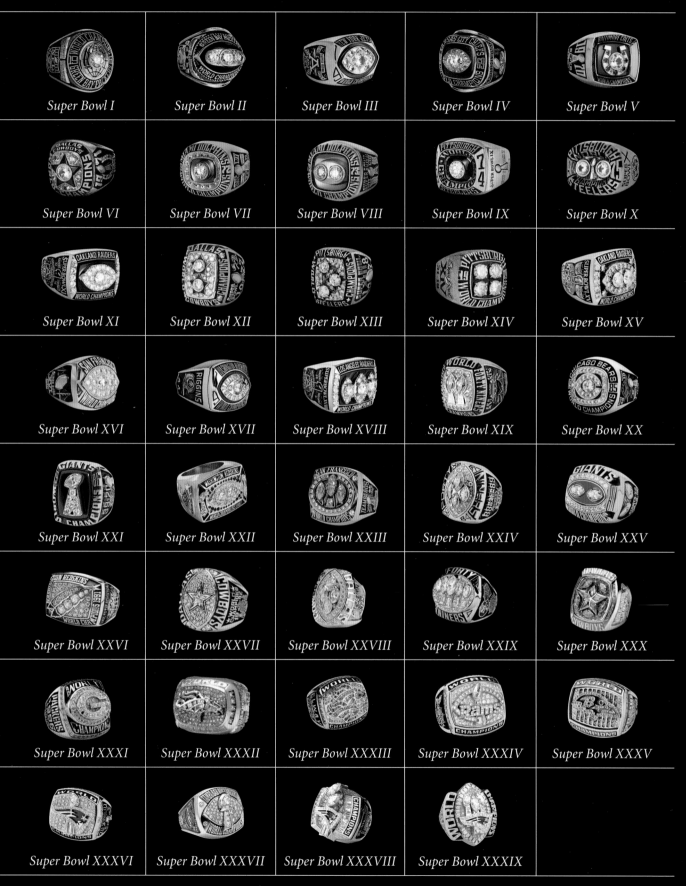

Super Bowl I

Super Bowl II

Super Bowl III

Super Bowl IV

Super Bowl V

Super Bowl VI

Super Bowl VII

Super Bowl VIII

Super Bowl IX

Super Bowl X

Super Bowl XI

Super Bowl XII

Super Bowl XIII

Super Bowl XIV

Super Bowl XV

Super Bowl XVI

Super Bowl XVII

Super Bowl XVIII

Super Bowl XIX

Super Bowl XX

Super Bowl XXI

Super Bowl XXII

Super Bowl XXIII

Super Bowl XXIV

Super Bowl XXV

Super Bowl XXVI

Super Bowl XXVII

Super Bowl XXVIII

Super Bowl XXIX

Super Bowl XXX

Super Bowl XXXI

Super Bowl XXXII

Super Bowl XXXIII

Super Bowl XXXIV

Super Bowl XXXV

Super Bowl XXXVI

Super Bowl XXXVII

Super Bowl XXXVIII

Super Bowl XXXIX